Common Core:
Re-Imagining the Music Rehearsal and Classroom

Standards, Curriculum, Assessment, Instruction

D1279645

Also by Paul Kimpton (with Delwyn Harnisch)

Scale Your Way to Music Assessment

Also by Paul Kimpton and Ann Kaczkowski Kimpton

Adventures with Music Series

Starting Early

Dog Tags

Summer of Firsts

COMMON CORE:

RE-IMAGINING
THE MUSIC REHEARSAL
AND CLASSROOM

STANDARDS, CURRICULUM, ASSESSMENT, INSTRUCTION

PAUL KIMPTON
AND ANN KIMPTON

THE PODIUM SERIES

GIA Publications, Inc.
Chicago

G-8765

GIA Publications, Inc.
7404 South Mason Avenue
Chicago, IL 60638
www.giamusic.com

Printed in the United States of America.

ISBN: 978-1-62277-101-1

CONTENTS

A CLARION CALL
FOR CHANGE

Teaching in the twenty-first century is a daunting yet exhilarating experience. It is daunting because a plethora of initiatives have been hurled at educators from every direction. The years of *No Child Left Behind*, with its narrow focus on reading and mathematics, standardized tests, and punitive measures toward "failing" schools, have been a difficult era for the arts. Funding for music programs has declined and schools have targeted the "Three R's" in an effort to boost student academic success as defined by student performance on multiple-choice tests in a variety of demographic areas. In this era of increased scrutiny of student achievement, the future of music in the schools could be in jeopardy, but only if music educators don't change. Current and future music educators will need to adapt their teaching philosophies, strategies, rehearsals, music selection processes, assessment practices, and grading procedures to justify one of the most important subjects a human can study—music!

The concept of half-life is an apt analogy for educators, as they struggle with how best to teach in today's schools. Half-life is defined as the time required for the activity of a substance taken into the body to lose one-half of its initial effectiveness. Consider that definition in terms of education and student learning. What is the effectiveness of what teachers teach if students forget half and are unable to make connections between music and their everyday lives or future careers? Why do students have difficulty with applying higher-level musical concepts independently? Several reasons exist. First, helping students understand the connection between the arts and everyday life and work has not been a focus of many music education programs, particularly performance-based classes. Next, students are not always engaged or held accountable to demonstrate, apply, analyze, evaluate, or create content or skills learned in meaningful, self-directed ways. Research suggests that when new concepts are connected to students' prior knowledge and applied in a variety of relevant ways, learning is more meaningful and longer lasting. And, that is the type of learning that is at the heart of the clarion call for change.

Movements such as the *21st Century Skills* and the *Common Core State Standards* herald the message for change. These two initiatives grew out of the need to elevate students' chances for success in a more complex society and will be discussed more in depth in later chapters in this book.

Let's face the facts. Each day there are fewer full-time jobs for musicians, be it teaching or performing. The population of arts donors and patrons is graying and music is losing its base of support. Furthermore, the students we teach are our legacy; they must see the value of music and how it adds to their lives—otherwise, why would they value and support music in the future?

The following quotation has strong implications for music educators:

*It is not the strongest of the species that survives, nor the most intelligent,
but the one most responsive to change.*

—Charles Darwin

Change is inevitable. I just read Brain Solis's book *What's the Future of Business?* The word "business" could be easily replaced with the word "school" or "music." Solis advocates that businesses that want to succeed must evolve and adapt to our changing world. Likewise, the purpose of *Common Core: Re-imagining the Music Rehearsal and Classroom* is to help music educators understand why change is necessary for the survival of music in our schools in the twenty-first century and to give teachers concrete examples about what that change could look like, be it performance-based or general music classrooms. Change will result in viable classes and self-directed musicians who understand the connection between the arts and everyday life. If we succeed, our students will be the ones to lead the charge to keep the future of music alive and well for generations to come. If we don't succeed, that's a future I would rather not contemplate. But, it's always darkest before the dawn, and as we move past this first decade of the Millennium, a light is beginning to shine.

REVELATION

People need revelation, and then they need resolution.

—Damian Lewis

When the Common Core State Standards were published in 2010, it took me two years to determine how to write this book. Along with many of my teaching colleagues, I just could not get a firm grasp of the Common Core State Standards and how music teachers and schools were going to implement them in effective ways while developing young musicians. I would examine the standards and consider how to apply them. I would talk to my wife, who is an assistant principal in charge of curriculum and instruction, hoping to hear the answers to my questions; whatever the reason, I was not able to internalize or grasp the steps from reading to application. What was I missing? Feeling frustrated, I decided to carry the documents in my briefcase, reviewing them when possible on my numerous travels that involved long periods of time alone in a car for thousands of miles, followed by climbing mountains and sitting with binoculars glassing spectacular waterfalls, forests, rock formations, elk, mule deer, bears, lakes, and the magnificent Canadian Rockies. I would consciously think about the documents occasionally, but subconsciously, my brain was probing, questioning, examining, analyzing, and evaluating.

Have you ever been doing something not related to your work, when suddenly you have a revelation and say, "I've got it?" Or, you wake up in the morning and realize you have solved a problem? We've all have had that happen at one time or another. What a magnificent feeling!

My revelation occurred in October 2012, at ten thousand feet in forty-degree weather as I sat glassing a mountain for elk, watching the sunrise over a beautiful snow-capped peak that reflected blue, pink, and white. I felt a shiver and thought it was the cold, but my mind told me differently. I was not even aware I was thinking about the Common Core State Standards, but I must have been, because I put my binoculars down and said out loud, "I've got it!" My guide Brian replied, "Where, I don't see it! Where are you looking?" Not wanting him to think I was crazy, I replied, "I don't see any game, but I just had an "aha moment." "I have devised an answer about how to implement the Common Core State Standards into the music classroom that I have been thinking about for two years." Brian just sat there for a minute, then replied, "A revelation, yah eeh....Well, good?" Bringing his glasses up, he continued to scan the mountains and valleys. I didn't reply, but I felt a sense of excitement and relief. Are you asking yourself what was the realization? It was that the Common Core State Standards are meant for teachers to stop teaching content that is a mile wide and an inch deep, and to have students understand our content and reach a level of understanding in a much deeper and meaningful way while enhancing and reinforcing the music we teach. I also realized it was not a book about the Common Core, it was a book about *teaching* and all the incredible elements in music that students need to understand to create music on a very high level and the variety of ways in which they can be taught and learned. Accordingly, the chapters in this book will simplify the Common Core into a manageable and applicable process for "teaching" music in meaningful and powerful ways. That one statement—a mile wide and an inch deep—opened my mind to the notion that there are so many other ways to inspire students to appreciate music, develop a deeper understanding and take responsibility to improve those skills. It is time to look at teaching from the podium in new ways and create in students greater musical skills who are independent learners. This book is about transforming a written document (the Common Core State Standards) into practical application in the music classroom. So, imagine you are on a mountaintop on a beautiful morning and are having a revelation. Join Ann and me in our revealing journey as you learn to apply the Common Core State Standards and thus energize your teaching and transform the student learning in your classroom.

ACKNOWLEDGMENTS

No one who achieves success does so without acknowledging the help of others.
The wise and confident acknowledge this help with gratitude.

—Alfred North Whitehead

The above quote is a perfect way to begin to thank the people who have helped change my thinking about music education and my place in it. They challenged me to reflect on what I do, why I did it, who I am, and what I could become.

This book is the sum of my support group. Therefore, I want to give credit to the following people for their help and support along the way:

- To my parents who have passed away but live through the experiences they gave me;
- To the hundreds of teachers and administrators I have worked with, who helped mold me into the educator, writer, musician, and clinician I am today;
- To all my students for allowing me to help them reach their potential while they helped me reach mine;
- To my co-author of this book who is also the co-author of my life: to Ann for editing and rewriting our lives together for thirty-nine years;
- To Carroll Gonzo my editor at GIA Publications, Inc., and his wise suggestions; and,
- Last and most important, to Alec Harris at GIA Publications, Inc., who has seen the potential in these books and has provided support and encouragement over the years. And, kudos goes to his hard-working staff for their efforts in making available a variety of books containing relevant topics to music educators throughout the world.

A richer, fuller life through music.

—Paul Kimpton

I would like to add to Paul's list of mentors who have helped us during our journey in education.

- To my father, Henry Kaczkowski, who supported his family with his paper route during the Depression and was able to earn a doctorate in education after WWII because of the financial benefits of the GI Bill for veterans.
- To my mother, MaryAlyce Hornby Kaczkowski, who, as with her father and mother, became an educator and nurtured her children to love learning.
- To the educators I have met along the way for their insight and wisdom.

—Ann Kimpton

How to Use This Book

The co-authors, along with the staff at GIA Publications, Inc., have made every effort to provide music educators with a wealth of information and material for creating, understanding, and implementing the Common Core State Standards into your music program, thereby making music the focus in the teaching/learning paradigm.

Support groups are important for music educators who often feel isolated. As you read this book, the message board at our Web site (www.mpae.net) allows you to post a question that will be answered by the authors in addition to giving other educators a chance to respond to your questions. Many schools are doing great things with assessment, 21st Century Skills, and the Common Core State Standards, and you will find you are not alone. Our Web site also has a list of dates and times when you may call and talk to Paul or Ann Kimpton for further discussion. As you work through each chapter, please share your questions and experiences, because our community of learners and we may help you on your journey to implementing the Common Core State Standards. All the blackline masters and material used will be available to you in Word files so you may edit and adjust the forms to your school's needs. If you would like a copy, please e-mail me at pkimpton@ mpae.net and tell me where you bought the book, where you teach, and the grade level. We will then send you a zip file of all the materials free.

Common Core: Re-imagining the Music Rehearsal and Classroom is designed to be used in many different ways and targets four distinct communities: music education professors; K–16 music educators; pre-service music educators; and school administrators.

Music Education Professors

Implementing the Common Core into the methods and music rehearsal as teaching strategies is an effective tool at the higher education level and will connect past- and present-teaching methods. If colleges and universities use a variety of teaching techniques with their students, major benefits can be realized. The music education students will witness first-hand how instructors are implementing current educational trends (the Common Core State Standards) into classrooms and rehearsals to enhance musical skills and understanding. Students know and understand only what they are exposed to, and the colleges and universities can be the leaders of change. College music educators are going to train the next generation of music educators; therefore, connecting music teaching to the Common Core in the classroom with actual teaching strategies that can be duplicated in their future classrooms must be a major goal. This book can also be used as a textbook in music methods classes. The chapters are specifically written to foster discussions and promote the design of student-focused teaching techniques that will be used from the first day of teaching forward. Other areas of use for *Common Core: Re-imagining the Music Rehearsal and Classroom* in a music education methods class may include how to:

- implement teaching techniques based upon best practice;
- change a culture;
- write specific learning targets;
- teach students how to write specific goals;
- use data to adjust instruction;
- motivate students;
- use data to provide feedback to students in areas of strength and weakness;
- use student feedback to improve instruction;
- create a culture of learning;
- manage time effectively;
- use blackline masters; and
- develop student accountability.

K-16 MUSIC EDUCATORS

The second community involves current K-16 music educators, the front-line troops in the battle to save music education. These educators face ever-growing pressure to expand grading in the classroom that promotes and measures a student's intellectual, emotional, and musical growth. A music educator who designed ways to implement the Common Core and a secondary administrator who worked closely with music teachers wrote this book. Teachers will be able to apply the material directly to their teaching and evaluation practices and begin to see the results in their students' skill development and growth. By following the steps set forth in this book, a district could adapt these ideas to their particular schools and communities without having to "start from scratch." Other areas of use for *Common Core: Re-imagining the Music Rehearsal and Classroom* in a music education methods class may include how to:

- implement teaching techniques based upon best practice;
- change a culture;
- write specific learning targets;
- teach students how to write specific goals;
- use data to adjust instruction;
- motivate students;
- use data to provide feedback to students in areas of strength and weakness;
- use student feedback to improve instruction;
- create a culture of learning;

- manage time effectively;
- develop student accountability;
- connect music to other disciplines;
- understand music selection as educational units;
- justify your music program to the school community;
- use blackline masters; and
- use writing to support and enhance musical understanding.

PRE-SERVICE MUSIC EDUCATORS

The third community, the music educators of the future, is the most important group of all. Young educators who enter their field often have limited exposure to teaching techniques that support a variety of learning styles employed in music programs in other schools. This narrow experience often results in first-year teachers trying to duplicate their high school or college experiences. *Common Core: Re-imagining the Music Rehearsal and Classroom* provides novice teachers with another model to consider when designing concerts and teaching musical skills and understanding. Young educators have a tough job indeed, often having ensembles perform just weeks after the opening of school. Furthermore, they must teach students how to improve individual musical skills. *Common Core: Re-imagining the Music Rehearsal and Classroom* will get them to improve quickly through taking responsibility for learning the skills they need in a variety of ways, thus creating a system that is applicable and supported by administrators. *Common Core: Re-imagining the Music Rehearsal and Classroom* for pre-service or novice teachers may include how to:

- implement teaching techniques based upon best practice;
- change a culture;
- write specific learning targets;
- teach students how to write specific goals;
- use data to adjust instruction;
- motivate students;
- use data to provide feedback to students in areas of strength and weakness;
- use student feedback to improve instruction;
- create a culture of learning;
- manage time effectively;
- develop student accountability;
- connect music to other disciplines;
- understand music selection as educational units;
- justify your music program to the school community;
- use blackline masters; and
- use writing to support and enhance musical understanding.

ADMINISTRATORS

The last community, administrators, is one that must not be neglected, since they hold the key to the future of music education in the schools. With diminishing budget resources and greater accountability to state and/or national standards and assessments, administrators face decisions about how to divvy up the funds. *Common Core: Re-imagining the Music Rehearsal and Classroom* will help music educators justify their programs as being an integral part of the curriculum, teaching crucial skills that may not be taught in any other discipline but can be educationally connected to other disciplines.

Developing a solid connection between the Common Core and other disciplines through music based upon current best practices will show that music can and does play a valuable role in a child's development. This book will also help administrators who have no previous experience in music to understand the components of a strong music program that is student centered and based upon encouraging students to develop musical skills in a variety of ways. Other uses of *Common Core: Re-imagining the Music Rehearsal and Classroom* may include how your music faculty can:

- implement teaching techniques based upon best practice;
- change a culture;
- write specific learning targets;
- teach students how to write specific goals;
- use data to adjust instruction;
- motivate students;
- use data to provide feedback to students in areas of strength and weakness;
- use student feedback to improve instruction;
- create a culture of learning;
- manage time effectively;
- develop student accountability;
- connect music to other disciplines;
- understand music selection as educational units;
- justify your music program to the school community;
- use graphic organizers; and
- use writing to support and enhance musical understanding.

CHAPTER 1
A BACKGROUND: 21ST CENTURY SKILLS
AND THE COMMON CORE STATE STANDARDS

THE MOVEMENT FOR REFORM

During the early portion of this century, a movement developed that particularly speaks to the arts: the Partnership for 21st Century Skills, aka P21. In 2002, the U.S. Department of Education provided matching funds to create a partnership of business, community, education leaders, and policymakers with the intention of creating a dialogue about the skills students would need for the future. This forward-thinking group was able to identify core subject areas and content that students should master, in addition to learning and thinking skills, information and communication technology literacy, and life skills that will prepare students to thrive in a global economy.

Fast forward to June of 2009 when two groups, the National Governors Association (NGA) and state educational leaders who made up the Council of Chief State School Officers (CCSSO), came together to establish a set of national standards. These standards would ensure that all students would be college or career ready by the time they graduated from high school. Prior to this monumental reform effort, each state had determined its own set of standards, and what students were expected to learn often varied widely from state to state. This independence in developing, adopting, and implementing standards created additional problems when states wanted to collaborate on policies, develop shared textbooks, or create common assessments and staff development programs. As a result, the Common Core State Standards were born.

It was the intent of the NGA and CCSSO to develop a common set of academic standards that would provide consistency in goals and expectations initially for English language arts and mathematics for all students across the nation. These two areas were selected because reading and math are what hold schools accountable to the federal government according to the federal law, No Child Left Behind (NCLB). As a result of this legislation, schools are required to measure students' progress in reading and math, and report the results that determine whether each school is considered "failing," which means that the number of students in that school fail to meet or exceed state standards on state tests.

The governors and state educational leaders needed help to develop this new set of standards, however, so they brought in teachers and educational experts as part of the task force to design common standards that states would share. The first public draft of the standards was made available in 2010, and at this point, forty-five states have adopted the Common Core as the standards for their students. The intent of the standards is not to dictate how teachers teach; rather, they provide the knowledge and skills that students should be expected to master at each grade level. The Partnership for 21st Century Skills acknowledges that its vision for articulating a set of skills and knowledge for core content areas is being realized through the development of the Common Core State Standards. Currently, the common standard movement has spread to other disciplines. For example, science is developing its Next Generation Science Standards and the arts are coming to consensus about standards that should be embraced nationally in arts education. A draft of the National Core Music Standards has been released, and clearly, these standards have been influenced by current movements that call for a transformation of education in America.

Our focus in this book is to illustrate the need for resulting change in music education, and why music educators should embrace the Common Core State Standards, in addition to high-quality, purposeful instructional and assessment design. We will demonstrate how music teachers can transform the performance classroom by implementing a strategic curricular design that can develop the students' musical understanding and performance skills. This design, in turn, will set the foundation for a strong music program and validate music's value as a curricular subject that reinforces the skills, knowledge, and expertise students must master to succeed in work and life. In order to better understand the Common Core State Standards, obtain a copy from your school or go to www.corestandards.org and print out the documents that we will be discussing throughout the book. Although the main focus of this book is the Common Core State Standards, it would be prudent for music educators to examine the twenty-first-century skills in Appendix A, because many of the skills students will need can be finely tuned in the music classroom.

CHAPTER 2
THE COMMON CORE STATE ENGLISH LANGUAGE ARTS STANDARDS AND MUSIC

WHAT ARE THE COMMON CORE STANDARDS FOR ENGLISH LANGUAGE ARTS?

Although the English Language Arts Common Core State Standards (www.corestandards.org) include standards that address speaking and listening skills in addition to language or grammatical skills, this book focuses on the standards in reading, writing, and mathematics, and how they can be addressed in the music classroom. The creators of the standards intended them to be implemented across the curriculum; regardless of the discipline, the communication arts are necessary and high-leverage skills for success in today's world.

The anchor standards at all grade levels are similar and spiral in complexity up through high school. The teaching of reading and writing are meant to be integrated with writing often used as an assessment of reading skills in the content area. The following are the grade 9-10 standards, but teachers will note the strong similarity at 11-12 and 6-8.

ENGLISH LANGUAGE ARTS COMMON CORE ANCHOR STANDARDS IN READING

KEY IDEAS AND DETAILS

1. Read closely to determine what the text says explicitly and to make logical inferences from it; cite specific textual evidence when writing or speaking to support conclusions drawn from the text.
2. Determine central ideas or themes of a text and analyze their development; summarize the key supporting details and ideas.
3. Analyze how and why individuals, events, and ideas develop and interact over the course of a text.

CRAFT AND STRUCTURE

1. Interpret words and phrases as they are used in a text, including determining technical, connotative, and figurative meanings, and analyze how specific word choices shape meaning or tone.
2. Analyze the structure of texts, including how specific sentences, paragraphs, and larger portions of the text (e.g., a section, chapter, scene, or stanza) relate to each other and the whole.
3. Assess how point of view or purpose shapes the content and style of a text.

INTEGRATION OF KNOWLEDGE AND IDEAS

1. Integrate and evaluate content presented in diverse formats and media, including visually and quantitatively, as well as in words.
2. Delineate and evaluate the argument and specific claims in a text, including the validity of the reasoning as well as the relevance and sufficiency of the evidence.
3. Analyze how two or more texts address similar themes or topics in order to build knowledge or to compare the approaches the authors take.

RANGE OF READING AND LEVEL OF TEXT COMPLEXITY

1. Read and comprehend complex literary and informational texts independently and proficiently.

ENGLISH LANGUAGE ARTS COMMON CORE ANCHOR STANDARDS IN WRITING

TEXT TYPES AND PURPOSES

1. Write arguments to support claims in an analysis of substantive topics or texts using valid reasoning and relevant and sufficient evidence.
2. Write informative/explanatory texts to examine and convey complex ideas and information clearly and accurately through the effective selection, organization, and analysis of content.
3. Write narratives to develop real or imagined experiences or events using effective technique, well-chosen details, and well-structured event sequences.

PRODUCTION AND DISTRIBUTION OF WRITING

1. Produce clear and coherent writing in which the development, organization, and style are appropriate to task, purpose, and audience.
2. Develop and strengthen writing as needed by planning, revising, editing, rewriting, or trying a new approach.
3. Use technology, including the Internet, to produce and publish writing and to interact and collaborate with others.

RESEARCH TO BUILD AND PRESENT KNOWLEDGE

1. Conduct short as well as more sustained research projects based upon focused questions, demonstrating understanding of the subject under investigation.
2. Gather relevant information from multiple print and digital sources, assess the credibility and accuracy of each source, and integrate the information while avoiding plagiarism.

3. Draw evidence from literary or informational texts to support analysis, reflection, and research.

RANGE OF WRITING

1. Write routinely over extended time frames (time for research, reflection, and revision) and shorter time frames (a single sitting or a day or two) for a range of tasks, purposes, and audiences.

WHY SHOULD MUSIC EDUCATORS EMBRACE THESE STANDARDS?

Music educators should embrace the Common Core State Standards for several reasons. First, they connect music educators to the school community. Music educators are seen as contributing to student skills that are measured by state and national tests or valued for preparing students for future careers. Music teachers can become leaders in their school and conversant with current educational trends.

Next, reading and writing offer opportunities for music students to reflect and set goals, thus improving attainment of musical skills. Reinforcing these skills also allows students to become independent learners, able to take on tasks without the dependence on a teacher to dispense information. Mastery of these skills opens worlds to students, teaches perseverance and the value of hard work, all skills valued in music.

Chapter 3
Rethinking the Rehearsal and the Music Classroom

Think is a powerful word. Type **think** into a thesaurus and the synonyms that appear are: contemplate, ponder, consider, imagine, envision, cogitate, reflect, reason, speculate, and deliberate. At no time do words such as destroy, terminate, kill off, or ruin appear among synonyms for the word "think." Nor does any negative connotation appear when we look at the prefix "re," which means go back. All we want you to do is to look with an open mind and consider this idea. At this time and place in history, is it time to rethink what we do as music educators and why.

Earlier in the book in the section titled *A Clarion Call*, the concept of half-life is discussed. Let's look at the half-life of a music performance class. Focusing on just school performance classes (band, orchestra, and choir) will help to narrow the parameters of our discussion.

Schools have had music programs, excluding bands, before 1912, but they weren't accredited subjects at that time. During the time between 1912 and roughly 1927, the majority of schools began giving credit for music, including band. If we use 1927 as a date where schools acknowledged music programs with credit, then we have had essentially ninety years of music classes that have been similar in structure then and now. By similar structure, we mean that a trained music teacher conducted student performance groups from a podium for the purpose of exposing students to music and giving concerts. It is fair to say that the main purpose over the past years of performing groups is to play and/ or sing music at concerts either in the school setting or at an event outside the school environment.

The main point of this book is: as educators we need to re-think the music rehearsal and the classroom that encompasses all aspects of teaching music. Let's begin our journey into rethinking the music classroom.

Take a minute to write down a few of the differences between 1927 and the present. Consider family structure, radios, TVs, phonographs, phones, lights, bathrooms, types of professions, white collar, blue collar, urban versus rural, school-sponsored sports, school-sponsored activities, movies, graduation rates from high school and college, just to name a few areas. Brainstorm your ideas and write them in one of the columns that follows. The list does not need to be comprehensive, but rather a starting point for a conversation. When you finish, discuss your list with a colleague.

1927	Present

Now let's go one step further. List the things that have not changed, keeping your focus on the classroom this time. You might list, for example, school day structure, method books, conducting, five-minute passing periods, music literature, etc.

1927 and the Present

Now that you are done, share your list with a colleague BUT DO NOT TURN IT INTO A DISCUSSION ABOUT THE GOOD OLD DAYS. Those days are gone forever. Discuss the present and future only. Keep it focused on what has not changed. There is no doubt you will have a lively discussion.

I hope that you see from your lists that the world has changed, but basically music performance and general music have not evolved to any great extent. Yes, we have better tuners, software to write music, music stands with computer screens that replace paper, computer software to play into that gives students feedback, access to a wealth of digital music and other innovations, but the basic idea of teaching students to perform music—regardless of the technology—has not changed what we teach from the podium or in our classrooms.

This lack of evolution is not singular to music. Education, on the whole, is slow to change. Many schools still embrace the lecture-discussion model with few assessments that ask the students to apply or demonstrate their knowledge in high-level, culminating performances. And, since the educational environment in the classroom has been slow to evolve, we are seeing a call for change from all sides. Let's not put the blame on any one group as demanding change, but a large part of the world wants accountability, innovative thinking, more in-depth thinking and real-world application because they are not seeing the change occurring from the bottom up. And, since they are not seeing change and have the power to create change, they are resorting to demanding change from the top down. If we don't initiate the change, someone else will. Read the quote below and write a short response.

Change before you have to.

—Jack Welch, former CEO of General Electric

_____

_____

_____

_____

This quote is relevant to the world we teach in today. We have not changed and now we HAVE TO. But is that bad? Continue to explore the benefits of opening our minds about change by responding to the next several statements: jot down a short reaction to the following statements:

- What new educational strategy have you initiated without being asked?
- Name the last book you have read on change in education or business that was not required by a class.
- Did you apply any of what you read?
- Is your style of teaching music or rehearsal based upon your experience with previous teachers?
- Why do you select the music you play or sing?
- What is better: to play eight songs with little understanding or musicality OR to play five songs with greater insight, musicality, and student engagement?
- Does your administration dictate how many songs you play on a concert?

- Do you teach by rote (repeating material with little student accountability)?
- What percentage of your students can play or sing all the music in a concert?
- How do you know what the percentage is?
- Do you have vocal or instrumental students in your school who cannot read or practice music on their own?

_____

_____

_____

_____

_____

PAUSE

Are you thinking, *what is the purpose of all these questions and discussions about change?* or are you thinking, *I thought this book was about applying the Common Core State Standards to enhance musical understanding and performance skills.*

PAUSE

If you are thinking any of those thoughts, then I have succeeded in getting you to see that in order to implement the strategies and ideas in this book, you are going to have to change how you think and teach. When you do, your students will become self-directed players and singers, will have a deeper understanding and appreciation of music, and will be able to connect the skills used in developing musicianship to their everyday lives, but what about you?

As a director, you will have focused rehearsals and the ability to reinforce the connection between music and life skills, to connect your subject to other subjects, and time to work on musicality not just "fixing notes." Additionally, you will have students who are held accountable for musical skills, who can independently learn and practice music, and can demonstrate high levels of musical understanding individually in performance situations. The most important result of implementing these changes is that you will begin to enjoy your work and will have a renewed sense of purpose.

WHY YOU TEACH THE WAY YOU DO

I think we are a product of all our experiences.

—Sanford I. Weill

Why you teach the way you do is one of the easiest, yet most difficult, questions to answer. First, who you are? You are the result of years of experiences and interactions with people from the time you were born. But, herein lies the problem. Some of us had better teachers, parents, interactions, travel, books, schools, education, instruments, and musical experiences than others. With that in mind, what would you or your teaching style be like if you had different interactions? Here is an interesting question to get you to think about why you teach the way you do. Take a few minutes and write or discuss your answer to the following question before reading further.

What if Michael Jordon had never touched a basketball?

_____

_____

_____

_____

_____

This question is one that I have asked students and teachers. The resulting conversations begin our journey into understanding who we are. Students and teachers begin to understand that their lives are a series of experiences and interactions, and that Michael Jordon would still be Michael Jordon but not the one we know. We teach the way we do because that is what we know. We are our experiences, and now we need to expand our experiences to consider implementing assessments and the Common Core State Standards into our teaching and our students' experiences. Remember the Michael Jordon question, and consider how we and our students might be different if we experience music in a new and exciting way.

Experience is the teacher of all things.

—Julius Caesar

WHAT IS THE REAL PURPOSE OF YOUR CURRICULUM?

Before answering the question above, let me give you my answer after having examined literally hundreds of school music programs. The majority of curricula are confusing, unused documents that are time-consuming, vague, unconnected to what is really going on from day to day in the music classroom, immeasurable, and never seen by students or parents. The teachers who wrote them were required to do so by administrators, but many are not held accountable for implementing or continually updating those documents. Furthermore, they rarely address the bigger picture of connecting in meaningful ways the study of music to other disciplines. If what you just read sounds familiar, then it is time to change.

Now, answer the question: What is the purpose of your music curriculum? Then discuss your answers with your colleagues.

WHAT IS THE REAL PURPOSE OF YOUR CONCERTS?

As I work with music departments around the country, teachers confuse the word curriculum with concerts. That means whatever the songs that are being prepared for the next concert, those songs and the musical skills that need to be taught to perform them are their curriculum. The director teaches from the podium, fixing mistakes and making no connection between music selection for a concert and the written curriculum. In addition, the songs are often chosen without matching current individual musical skills and prepping the students for learning the new skills needed to perform the piece. If directors do not match or prep the students' skills to the music, then the rehearsals are often tense, unproductive, repetitive, and inefficient, never reaching a high level of musicality on the students' or groups' part. It is at this juncture that embracing the Common Core State Standards, along with summative and formative assessments, will help you to change the way you select and teach music in your classroom. In the later chapters of this book, you will see how graphic organizers and a variety of teaching strategies can enhance your instruction of music.

ASSESSMENT

If you have read *Scale Your Way to Music Assessment* and *Grading for Musical Excellence*, you will have a better understanding about how individual and group assessments are used to measure and guide your teaching methods. When the word assessment is used, we will assume you have a fairly reasonable understanding about how assessments are developed and implemented. If not, I will provide a short overview of each area discussed, even though the topic of assessment is a book in itself. To create a meaningful music experience, a teacher needs to understand where the students are and where they need to get to both individually and as a group. Assessment of skills is not only necessary for the students, but also the teacher. Students must take responsibility for learning and mastering the skills that are valued, and teachers are responsible for giving students feedback based upon formative and summative assessments so that students can make progress toward attaining mastery of skills.

The Common Core State Standards encourage a high-level demonstration of those skills. Having a strong background in assessment will be further supported through using a variety of written, listening, and performance assessments to measure that growth. Additionally, the connection between reading and writing skills and their ability to strengthen student musical skills will be discussed.

Let's face it. What most conductors want are better players, singers, and performances, and by opening yourself up to new ways of developing and reinforcing those skills through the Common Core State Standards, you will be able to achieve Independent Musicians Creating Quality Performances.

VALUE OF CHANGE

> *Don't limit a child to your own learning,*
> *for he was born in another time.*
>
> —Rabindranath Tagore

Being able to accept change while maintaining the core essence of music performance is the primary purpose of this book. Before we begin our in-depth understanding of the Common Core State Standards, I would like to expose you to a book called *Flying Without a Net, Turn Fear of Change into Fuel for Success* by Thomas J. Delong. The book originally was written for business executives, but it has far-reaching implications for teachers and administrators. Let me start by sharing a story from the book. "I was addressing a group of high school principals, and after the talk, one of them approached and thanked me. The principal said, 'Professor Delong, I'm forty-three years old, and I find my job frustrating and not enjoyable at all. But the good news is that I only have twelve years until retirement.'" Does this sound familiar? Numerous times at conventions and workshops, I have heard this same comment from music educators. Let's see how Professor Delong responded.

"I didn't know how to reply. But, I wanted him to understand that if he is going to be an effective leader who inspires and guides his students he needs to get past his fears and frustration, his routines and rituals. He needs to be more bold rather than more conservative, more willing to experiment rather than preserve the status quo, more open to fresh ideas and new educational technologies rather than adhering to fear and failure as motivations."

The book continues to explore why we don't change and why we should. A phrase that hit home to me was "Doing the right thing poorly." The premise is that if you want to follow a path to growth, you can't avoid the stage, where you are vulnerable. Instead of staying the same, you might go through a phase of "doing the right thing poorly "on your way to "doing the right thing well."

Write your reactions to the idea of being vulnerable.

_____

_____

_____

_____

_____

Now that you are thinking about change, let's do two more exercises. I want to share a concept/activity developed by Phil Daniels, a professor at Brigham Young University, which is also discussed in *Flying Without a Net*. It is called SKS. It is a process whereby we should ask others what we should *stop* (S), *keep* (K), and *start* (S) doing. You can do this with other teachers, administrators, students, or spouses, always limiting entries to three comments on each area. After creating your lists, discuss the following questions:

1. What should I stop doing?
   - Are you hearing that you should quit doing something that you believe is a skill or strength?
   - Is your first response that discontinuing this behavior will have catastrophic consequences?
   - On reflection, is it possible that you've fallen into a behavior rut? If you stop doing one thing, might you have an opportunity to try something new and different?

2. What should I keep doing?
   - Is there something you're doing right that people think you should do more of?
   - Have you been dismissive of this particular behavior or skill for some reason?
   - What might happen if you used this "Keep" more? How might it impact your effectiveness and satisfaction with your job?

3. What should I start doing?
   - Are people recommending you do something that feels foreign or scary?
   - What about it makes you anxious? Is it because you are afraid of looking like you don't know what you're doing?
   - Why are people suggesting you start doing this new thing? What benefits do they feel will accrue to you, your group, or your organization?

The last exercise to begin thinking about changing was developed by Ann Harriet Bucks for people who feel stuck and experience psychological paralysis. These people need to think of opposites. The implications from these statements are not only for teachers, but also for students.

- If you have been sitting, stand.
- If you have been standing, sit.
- If you have been traveling, stay home.
- If you have been home, travel.
- If you have been teaching, learn.
- If you have been learning, teach.
- If you have been talking, listen.
- If you have been listening, talk.

If we translate this advice, it might look similar to the statements below.

- If you have been playing it safe, take a risk.
- If you have been only working on tasks with which you're comfortable, take on a discomforting assignment.
- If you have been only listening to a small circle of advisors, bring in outsiders.
- If you have been focusing on short-term goals, think long term.

What opposites would you consider? List a few below.

_____

_____

_____

_____

_____

I want to congratulate you for reading this far and keeping an open mind. The fact that you are opening your mind to new ideas is fantastic. The above exercises have begun to encourage you to look at not only your teaching life, but also your personal and family life because we know as teachers they all interact. As we continue our journey together in the next chapters, I will continue to challenge you and refer back to the notion that change is good.

CHAPTER 4
MUSIC IS DESCRIBED AS A UNIVERSAL LANGUAGE, BUT WHAT'S THE CONNECTION TO READING AND WRITING?

Music is often described as a universal language, one that crosses cultural boundaries. Language is a way to communicate meaning, to convey emotions, to articulate ideas. Unlike language that may be specific to a region and be unintelligible to a person unfamiliar with the vocabulary and syntax, music can speak to and be understood by a diverse audience.

If music and language both are used to communicate, how can one understand that their similarities and differences impact instruction in the music classroom? A closer examination of the commonalities of music and language will serve as a framework for a discussion of how to guide students toward high levels of proficiency in both domains.

SYMBOL/SOUND RELATIONSHIP

Both music and language have a written form that connects a symbol to a sound. In language that relationship is called phonemic awareness, a time when children begin to realize that the words people say are connected to symbols on a page. That squiggly line that looks like a snake is called an "S" and sounds like "ess." Some children develop this conceptual knowledge intuitively or as a result of being exposed to print at an early age, whereas other children learn from explicit instruction in the rules of the sound/symbol relationships, that which we call phonics. For years, reading instructors have argued over the benefits of whole language—teaching how symbols form sounds more in context—versus direct instruction in phonics. In the 1950s and 1960s, a focus on phonics resulted in school children across America completing worksheets that had them fill in before the word "at," "b," "c," or "h" and so on to learn that various consonants combined with a short "a" and "t" formed "bat," "cat," and "hat."

What does an understanding of the struggle to teach the relationship between letters, words, and sounds mean for music educators? First, it helps to reinforce the view that all children do not learn to read music in the same way. Some children may have a more intuitive understanding that notes on a page represent keys on a piano or fingerings on a clarinet. Those children may benefit from an emphasis on the big picture—in other words, they can learn note names and rhythms in context while they play or sing a piece. Other children, however, may need more direct instruction in developing that conceptual understanding. Those children may learn better by starting with the details of note names, whole notes, and half notes before putting them together to play or sing a whole piece. Music educators must develop a balanced approach to teaching that plays to the individual strengths of their students.

Next, reading educators also know that the younger a child is exposed to text and develops an awareness of print, the easier it will be to teach that child to read. Thus, many national programs emphasize reading to children as early as possible. Music educators should promote listening to a variety of music, including classical, as early as possible in a child's life. Elementary music teachers could provide a list of suggested pieces or songs to listen to, much like libraries have suggested reading lists. With today's technology, any song is only a click away on iTunes.

LITERAL/INFERENTIAL COMPREHENSION

Music and language also depend upon literal comprehension, or what is on the page, and inferential comprehension, or what is between the lines or unstated directly. As students mature in their competencies to sing or play, and as the books or music they read become more complex, the time spent teaching shifts from more literal interpretation of the music—students learn to play the notes, the dynamics, the rhythms exactly as stated directly on the page—to developing skills in musical interpretation and expressiveness, the ability to make inferences as reading educators call it.

DEVELOPING LITERAL AND INFERENTIAL SKILLS IN THE MUSIC CLASSROOM

ILLUSTRATION 1

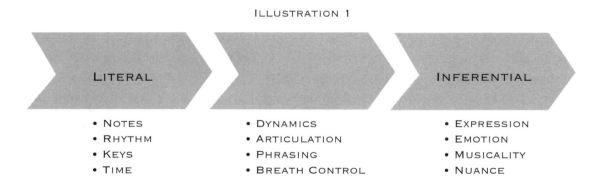

LITERAL	DYNAMICS	INFERENTIAL
• NOTES	• DYNAMICS	• EXPRESSION
• RHYTHM	• ARTICULATION	• EMOTION
• KEYS	• PHRASING	• MUSICALITY
• TIME	• BREATH CONTROL	• NUANCE

Whether it is text or music, literal comprehension is the ability to interpret what's on the page. Too often, educators at all levels get stuck in teaching at the literal level, never getting to a more complex, higher-level understanding of the text. Many times this inability to get to the inferential level is because the text is too difficult or students lack the background knowledge and allusions to references that ease the ability to comprehend. Text used in the classroom can be divided into three levels: independent, instructional, and frustrational. When selecting books for the classroom, teachers look for texts that are at students' instructional level, not too difficult, nor too easy, but that, with some assistance by the teacher, can be accessed by the class.

Music educators can learn from this similarity to reading by realizing that music selection, as with text selection, is crucial to a successful classroom or performance ensemble. Students will never get to the interpretive level of playing or singing music if the music is too difficult and the students cannot play at the literal level. Knowing student strengths and weaknesses is crucial; selecting music that challenges students yet ensures that notes and rhythms are not at the level of frustration will allow instructors to have time to focus on musicality and expressiveness.

EXPRESSIVE AND RECEPTIVE CAPACITIES

The capacity to both receive and express communication is another commonality between music and language. Receptive language or the ability to understand or appreciate words or music precedes the ability to express. Usually, receptive capacities are at a higher level than those of expressive. For example, students can listen to music and may be able to understand the complexities of a piece of music far greater than their ability to produce that level of music. As with the other similarities, the more a student listens to and builds an aural library, the greater that student's capacity to be able to express more complex music.

THE ROLE OF EMOTIONAL COMMUNICATION

Both music and language tap into the emotional part of the brain, the limbic system that includes the amygdale, which allows humans to form emotions and the hypothalamus that deals with expression of emotions. The stimulation of emotion allows students to connect more deeply with music and language than with any other discipline. But, emotion without content knowledge and understanding is limiting and will not allow students to reach the heights of their potential. For example, when reading a poem, students may feel a basic emotional connection to the words, but when students have the content knowledge to understand the allusions, the figurative language, and how the structure of the verse supports the tension of the piece, then the emotional connection is heightened; just as when playing and/or singing a piece or listening to a composition, the emotional experience that occurs is intensified when the musician can appreciate the underlying structures that were artfully designed by the composer.

MOTIVATION AND PERCEPTION

Developing skill in music and language requires a certain amount of effort, and thus the development of skills in both areas necessitates motivation on the part of the student if a high level of competency is to be reached. Motivational research suggests that people are motivated by three basic desires, which will be referred to as the Three C's: control, competence, and connection. For more information on motivational research, and in particular, self-determination theory (SDT), please consult the extensive research by Edward Deci and Richard Ryan (2000). Through an understanding of these three desires, educators can better motivate students to put forth the effort it takes to attain the complex, higher-level skills demanded by the Common Core State Standards. Likewise, to attain a high level of skill development in music, students must persevere and spend many hours in practice—and that can only occur if a student is motivated. Music educators can enhance a student's motivation by appealing to one or more of the three C's.

The first C, "control," is a motivating factor for students because it gives them a feeling of power over their own destiny; if students feel they are invested in a task, that they have some sort of control over what is happening, they are more likely to be more motivated to do whatever it takes to accomplish the task. By allowing the students to have a sense of choice, such as selecting the music for a solo, deciding weak or strong skills to develop, or setting individual goals, there is going to be a greater sense of control, and thus motivation, to learn the music than if the music were handed down to the student. As with the individual student, an ensemble can also be motivated through "choice." If the group believes they are actively involved in the selection of goals to be accomplished during the semester and that they have a voice in the selection of music, they will be more motivated to immerse themselves more deeply in the subject and achieve those goals, not only individually, but also as a group.

Developing a sense of control is also a foundational principle of the Common Core State Standards in the sense that the high-level tasks that students will be asked to complete will involve a synthesis of multiple texts and development of opinions. Students will need to choose what they feel is important in a text and support that choice with evidence. Assessments will require more open-ended responses, thus giving students more freedom to generate their own responses with fewer forced choices among answers created by someone else. By appealing to a student's need for control, music educators can help the student to be more discriminating and purposeful and develop the skill of making choices that allow a student to be successful. And, that success will breed a desire for more success, thus creating a cycle of motivation for the student.

Underlying the next C, or "competence," is the theory that humans are driven by a desire to feel a sense of competence. Most people do not want to appear to be inept. Students do not want to be embarrassed by a lack of skill, especially in front of their peers. Some students will be naturally driven to become competent and will work diligently, motivated by their own internal need to be the best at a particular skill. These students are referred to as mastery-oriented in Bernard Weiner's attribution theory (1974, 1986). Other students are more complex, and are not so easily motivated by the desire for competence either through internal or external rewards. Although they may act as though they don't care, they may say to their peers that, "This is stupid," while inwardly, they really do want to be competent. These students often believe that talent in music is finite; either a person has musical talent, or he doesn't. They do not see the connection between hard work and the development of musical skills. According to the attribution theory, these students would be considered performance-oriented.

If we view students in our music classes as fitting into one of the attribution theory's two groups, mastery-oriented students would seek to *improve* their competence while performance-oriented students would seek to *prove* their competence. Students who are mastery-orientated would tend to see the value of practice and effort in learning a musical skill, whereas students who are performance-oriented would tend to see ability as finite—a person is either musically talented or not—and would not see the correlation of practice and effort with musical success.

The following chart developed by Marilla D. Svinicki delineates the characteristics of mastery-oriented students and performance-oriented students. *Student Goal Orientation, Motivation, and Learning* (Marilla D. Svinicki, 2005).

ILLUSTRATION 2

MASTERY VERSUS PERFORMANCE

Mastery-Oriented Students	Performance-Oriented Students
Main interest is in learning the skill/content.	Main interest is in appearing competent or better than others regardless of level achieved.
Is willing to take on difficult tasks beyond present capability.	Sticks to tasks that are familiar, known quantities.
Views mistakes as learning opportunities.	Views mistakes as evidence of lack of competence and therefore to be avoided.

The Common Core Standards are skewed toward students who are mastery-oriented. These students are willing to work diligently on difficult, complex tasks. They see mistakes as opportunities for growth. On the other hand, students with a performance orientation value the appearance of competence over in-depth learning. These students would rather select an easy solo rather than risk failure by taking on a more challenging piece. Their self-esteem is linked to the appearance of competence, and thus, to preserve that sense of self, they will avoid challenging situations that may make them think they are incompetent. If they are put in such a situation, they tend to downplay the event by intimating, "I could have played better if I had practiced." The defense of, "I didn't practice," becomes a crutch that allows students to maintain the perception of competence and avoid the feeling of, "What happens if I do practice, and I still fail? How can I keep my sense of competence if I try, but still can't attain a skill?" For these students, the easiest response is to give up: "That way, I can keep my sense of competence ("I really could do it, IF I wanted to") rather than believe, "I really have no musical talent because of my belief that a person either has it or he doesn't."

In the twenty-first century, more than any other time in previous decades, teachers will need to help students develop a mastery orientation toward learning and the motivation to take on challenging tasks. One way to support this view of learning in the music classroom is to continually connect a student's hard work and effort with achievement of skills. This connection will require, however, teachers to set up multiple opportunities to provide focused feedback to students about their progress toward musical skills and to demonstrate their in-depth understanding through a variety of means, be it playing, writing, reading, or speaking. Teachers should publically value risk-taking through encouraging students to take on challenging, though appropriate, music. They should continually point out the connection between effort and attainment of skills, praising small increments of movement toward gaining skills. If teachers reinforce this connection, students are able to change their orientation to one that lends itself more toward the high-level, in-depth learning demanded for success in today's world.

The final C is "connection." Students tend to be more motivated when they believe that what they are learning is connected to other areas of their lives and that they see the learning as having a connection or purpose for them. Teachers can play a major role by illustrating the connections between subject areas. For example, a focus on the Common Core literacy standards throughout the school—that reading, writing, listening, and speaking are ways of communicating that allow students to demonstrate at a high level their understanding—can help students make connections between subject areas. If students see that literacy skills are valued in more than one class, then they are more likely to be motivated to develop these skills that will serve them for a lifetime. One of the principles of the Common Core is the interdisciplinary relationship of subjects in a school. Schools cannot afford to teach subjects in silos without showing the inter-relatedness of the disciplines.

The final motivating factor of "connection" is the human one: that many students want to feel a connection with their teachers. This connection factor is a huge one in the music classroom because of the emotional connection students have with music and that they often have the same music teacher for many years. That's why it pays to get to know your students, to talk with them, not just about music, for they will "work their hearts out" for someone they like. And, having students like a teacher should not be confused with doing whatever the students want. Students want to learn, they want to develop skills, and they want to respect the teachers who will get them there. All in all, teachers should have high expectations for students, but if it is done in a way that students know you have their best interests at heart, that you care about them as people, then they will be motivated to persevere and take on the challenge of complex tasks.

CHAPTER 5
UNDERSTANDING THE MUSICAL PERFORMANCE PYRAMID

ILLUSTRATION 3

THE MUSICAL PERFORMANCE PYRAMID

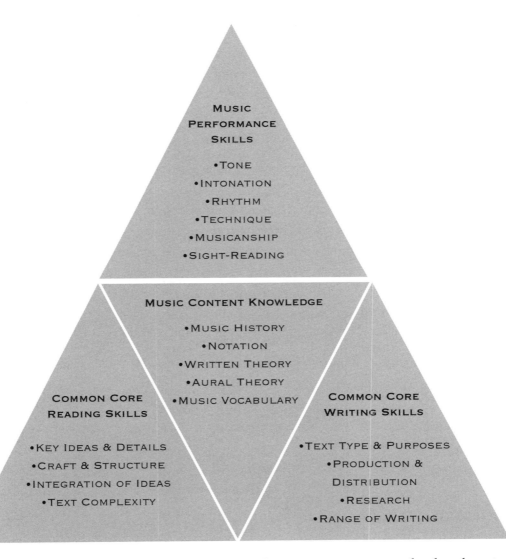

MUSIC
PERFORMANCE
SKILLS

- TONE
- INTONATION
- RHYTHM
- TECHNIQUE
- MUSICANSHIP
- SIGHT-READING

MUSIC CONTENT KNOWLEDGE

- MUSIC HISTORY
- NOTATION
- WRITTEN THEORY
- AURAL THEORY
- MUSIC VOCABULARY

COMMON CORE
READING SKILLS

- KEY IDEAS & DETAILS
- CRAFT & STRUCTURE
- INTEGRATION OF IDEAS
- TEXT COMPLEXITY

COMMON CORE
WRITING SKILLS

- TEXT TYPE & PURPOSES
- PRODUCTION &
  DISTRIBUTION
- RESEARCH
- RANGE OF WRITING

The above illustration indicates how skills in literacy support greater depth in learning in the music classroom. The Common Core State Standards for Reading and Writing allow students to learn in greater depth the music content knowledge that supports the performance skills. For example, for students to perform a piece with the proper technique and musicianship, they need to have an understanding of the historical framework of the piece: In what time period was the piece written? Who was the person who composed the music and how would that knowledge affect a performance of the composition? What historical events occurred that may have influenced the composer? How might knowledge of those events impact the musical interpretation of the piece? Furthermore, what musical vocabulary needs to be learned in order to perform the music.

Music teachers should build upon their students' foundational knowledge of story structure, how both a musical composition and story begin with an exposition or introduction and build toward a climax. They can connect how key ideas and major themes are introduced in both a story and a composition, and how an understanding of them lends itself to greater understanding of the piece overall, and thus an enhanced performance. All in all, without a strong base of literacy, it is nearly impossible to scale the pyramid to an enhanced musical performance.

ARE YOU ON THE PERFORMANCE TREADMILL?

Many music teachers may feel they are running on a never-ending treadmill of preparing for performances. Once the fall concert is over, there are holiday concerts, followed by winter concerts, large group contest, and spring performances. Just when directors have fixed all the mistakes and students perform the pieces for that concert, the next concert deadline looms in the future, and they are back on the treadmill of getting ready for the next concert. The cycle repeats itself next year, with the music educator feeling that there is never enough time to prepare for each performance, to fix all the mistakes, and that the easiest way to teach students is to have them learn pieces by rote. Any time spent developing a deeper understanding of the music is time that takes away from preparing for the next concert.

ILLUSTRATION 4
LEARNING CONTINUUM

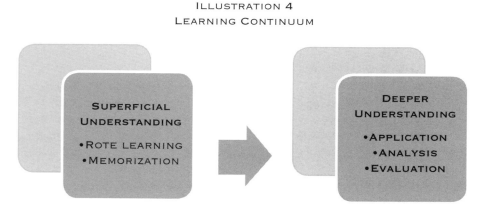

But, music instruction in the classroom doesn't have to be this way. As teachers, we can choose which side of the learning continuum we want to focus on. Do we want to be stuck on the performance treadmill with its narrow focus on superficial understanding of the music students play for a concert? Or do we want to move toward deeper understanding that allows our students to apply the skills they have learned, to analyze and evaluate their performance, and to create a truly satisfying musical experience for both themselves and the audience? Through strategic planning, instruction in the music classroom can be purposeful, highlighting student strengths while addressing student weaknesses. Student understanding will be deeper because daily instruction is focused on developing specific skills and content rather than a random series of error correction or superficial playing of literature.

Additionally, selection of music is a critical component for directors who want to move toward deeper student understanding on the learning continuum. Music selection must be intentional and based upon students having the appropriate skills so that students are able to demonstrate a deeper understanding of the music. When directors tailor their music selection toward student skills, students will be able to get to the music rather than just playing the notes. Moreover, directors should consider playing fewer pieces during each concert so that the music is played with greater understanding and musicality.

A concert program that is an inch deep and a mile wide serves no purpose other than to have an audience listen for hours to a mediocre performance. Strategic selection of concert repertoire will allow students to move toward the right side of the continuum and demonstrate musical performance skills at the highest level of understanding.

ILLUSTRATION 5
STUDENT PERFORMANCE/REFLECTIVE LOOP

To make progress toward goals, a student's role in the classroom must be clearly articulated. The Student Performance/Reflective Loop illustrates how teacher feedback, student reflection, and goal setting are interrelated with practice and performance. The cycle begins when students receive feedback from a performance. Once they process the feedback, students should reflect in writing and respond to the feedback. Writing is a critical part of the Student Performance/Reflective Loop because it develops student ownership and responsibility of their role in using feedback to improve performance. Because growth in musical skills takes time, having a written record also allows students to look back and see skill growth over time.

This part of the Student Performance/Reflective Loop also illustrates how the Common Core State Standards can support the development of skills in the performance arts. Writing Anchor Standard 1—ask students to present an argument claim and support it with evidence. For example, students may be asked, "Does the feedback you received match your perception of the performance? Do you feel the feedback is valid; if not, why? What steps will you now take to improve your skills for the next performance? If your skills are at an acceptable level, what new skills will you work on for the next cycle?" All these questions and more can be part of the initial reflection that asks students to form an opinion and support that opinion with evidence that they have observed. Through the articulation of this evidence, students will be better able to make the connection between the practice of skills and the resulting performance.

This initial reflection then leads to Step 2, goal setting, for the next series of practices. These practices are interspersed with opportunities for feedback from the teacher, additional time for reflection and, if necessary, adjustment of the original goals.

The ability to plan and adjust goals is a life skill for students, especially in music. Attending to this skill also addresses Common Core Writing Standard (W.CCR.4) by having students plan and reflect on their goals. Each concert or contest happens in real time and is usually accomplished in a set amount of time. Giving students the tools to write, plan, revise, and edit both long-term and short-term goals will accomplish two major objectives for performance.

1. Individual music parts will be learned in a timely manner, thus allowing your rehearsals to move from the superficial, corrective rehearsal to one that is focused on higher-level skills where the majority of rehearsal time is devoted to the emotion and expressiveness of the music.
2. Evaluation of student progress over a period of time will allow you to develop three types of assessments to be used to drive your rehearsal and your students' individual practice session.

   • Teacher to student assessment – This assessment is done on a one-to-one basis and not in rehearsal or performance. The director hears each selection to be performed individually and feedback is given immediately. This assessment accomplishes two very important goals. First, students cannot hide their efforts in developing the skills necessary to perform the selections; second, the teacher will have a better understanding of what the students are able to do, thus allowing the director to adjust the rehearsal and correct mistakes not heard from the podium.

- Student-to-student or peer assessment – This assessment is only possible after the teacher has demonstrated how to give proper feedback to students using musical terms and suggested corrections. The assessment can be done in writing from one student to another, further strengthening the connection between writing and music, or having each student play for the other can do it verbally or less formally. Then the pair can discuss what is working and what and how mistakes need to be corrected.

- Individual self-assessment – This assessment is by far the most crucial in building independent musicians. In order for the student to record himself or herself, and then listen critically, the student must have internalized the level of performance you desire. Moreover, he or she is able to look critically at his or her playing and make adjustments as a proactive routine to correct the errors. The director can model this behavior by reviewing and commenting on concerts, individual performances, and by creating an open, non-judgmental, risk-free assessment environment.

PLANNING SHEET

The planning sheet in Illustration 6 may be adjusted to your individual needs. The students are asked to plan their weekly practice schedule, assuming that they understand where they need to work and when you will hear them play. They are asked to give specific measures and use musical terminology about what needs to be done. When working with students, make it very clear that if they are not going to practice on a certain day, they should say so. They should learn that a plan is to be accomplished—not just to look good on paper and never implemented. It is important that they understand the limited time available in their busy lives, and thus, they need to be able to adjust how they practice by having focused practice time on specific weak areas. For a more detailed explanation of the process, please refer to *Scale Your Way to Music Assessment*, Chapters 8 and 9 and *Grading for Musical Excellence*, Chapters 5, 6, and 7.

ILLUSTRATION 6

PLANNING SHEET

This planning sheet should focus on what areas in the music you need to work on. Times and dates should be accurate. Please use music-specific language.

Name_____Due Date_____ Student ID_____

LUCK – There is no such thing as luck; only the ability to
LABOR – UNDER – CORRECT – KNOWLEDGE

Friday – Date_____Start Time_____End Time_____

Band/Perc./Ensemble/Solo/Lesson/Scale   Section/Measures What is the focus?

Saturday – Date_____ Start Time_____End Time_____

Band/Perc./Ensemble/Solo/Lesson/Scale   Section/Measures What is the focus?

Sunday – Date_____ Start Time_____End Time_____

Band/Perc./Ensemble/Solo/Lesson/Scale   Section/Measures What is the focus?

Monday – Date_____ Start Time_____End Time_____

Band/Perc./Ensemble/Solo/Lesson/Scale   Section/Measures What is the focus?

Tuesday – Date_____ Start Time_____End Time_____

Band/Perc./Ensemble/Solo/Lesson/Scale   Section/Measures What is the focus?

Wednesday – Date_____ Start Time_____End Time_____

Band/Perc./Ensemble/Solo/Lesson/Scale   Section/Measures What is the focus?

Thursday – Date_____ Start Time_____End Time_____

Band/Percussion./Ensemble/Solo/Lesson/Scale Section/Measures What is the focus?

WEEKLY REFLECTION SHEET

Now let's look at what makes the student Planning Sheet so powerful. The Weekly Reflection Sheet in Illustration 7 that is done at the end of the planned week is where the learning comes together. Students must look honestly at what they have accomplished, understanding that in a fixed time event, such as preparing for a concert, weekly progress must be achieved in order for the group and the individual to reach a high level of performance. Again, reaching the targeted goals is possible because the director has instructed students in the process of reviewing past progress and taking responsibility for readjusting their practice time for the next week based upon this week's progress. The teacher must read the students' plan and reviews to monitor their progress and ensure that they are writing what they are actually doing and not just what they think the teacher wants to read. Students should be given written feedback on the review and the plan, either weekly if possible or on some other consistent schedule. In the end, however, the teacher must respond to the students' writing in a timely manner.

ILLUSTRATION 7
WEEKLY REFLECTION

WEEKLY REFLECTION SHEET

Name_____ Date_____

Review sheets are designed for you to reflect back on your planning sheet to see if you have accomplished what you had written previously. Use this reflective time to review goals and gain insight into your weekly accomplishments.

You must have correct dates of missed goals, specific bars not worked on, and make-up work. Answers must be in-depth and not one-word answers.

The purpose of this assignment is for you to be honest with yourself and understand why you are or are not reaching your written goals. If you learn how to turn negative behavior into positive behavior, you will have a greater chance to reach your goals.

How many practice times did you schedule?_____

How many times did you actually practice?_____

If you missed some planned practice times – explain. Be specific.

List the sections in your music you need to work on for the next performance:
Title   Section/Measure   What is the focus?

Could you have planned better to reach this week's goals? Yes or No – Explain.

What will you do differently next week? You must be specific.

REHEARSAL REVIEW AND PLAN SHEET

This final Rehearsal Review and Plan Sheet in Illustration 8 is for both the director and the students. It is designed to further reinforce writing and correcting performance errors or, on a positive note, to reinforce strengths. The information on this sheet requires the students to write down what types of comments are being made from the podium. The director will need to demonstrate what that means by showing them a sample review in which musical comments are emphasized—not comments that are funny, sarcastic, or non-musical in nature. By writing down what is going on in rehearsal, the students and teacher can begin to see where precious rehearsal time is being spent. If it is on basic corrections, then who needs to take responsibility? If the students see they need to take responsibility, then they will start to focus their practice on correcting those areas so the group can move on. Students who never make corrections are what we call "rehearsal leeches" who pull the rehearsal and the group down to their level. Many teachers often teach to those students, ignoring the ones who are playing correctly. Teachers who have used this review sheet with their students have found that both students and teachers are able to see the rehearsal as something they all need to take responsibility for in making it a positive and musical experience.

By using Planning, Review, and Rehearsal Review Sheets, a director can use writing to improve both individual and group performance. Additionally, musical skills and knowledge can be assessed and strengthened and, as a result, musical performance enhanced. Each individual in the group is thus responsible for the musical experience.

ILLUSTRATION 8

REHEARSAL REVIEW AND PLAN SHEET

Name_____Date_____Week #_____

Title of Piece_____

The instructions are on the reverse side of this form.

Comments about correctives or basic musical skills

1.

2.

3.

Comments about higher-level musical understanding

1.

2.

3.

Based upon the comments above, are there areas that you should strengthen in your playing? If you need to take responsibility for moving the group from basic corrections to a higher-level, musically oriented rehearsal, what will you do this next week in your practice? Be specific in what measure or skill needs to be worked on.

1.

2.

3.

ILLUSTRATION 9

REHEARSAL REVIEW AND PLAN SHEET INSTRUCTIONS

A group's success is often the result of students and teachers working collaboratively to learn a piece of music. If both teacher and student review the rehearsal comments, either weekly on Friday or bi-weekly, the two can begin to see progress toward growth in skills. Students who hear repeated comments about notes, keys, fingerings, accents, dynamics, bowing, etc., must realize that these basic musical skills are their job to correct once the director has provided feedback. Not making those corrections in a timely manner creates tense and unproductive rehearsals. And vice-versa—if directors realize they continually are making the same corrections, then a different approach to solving the problem must be employed.

This review sheet will help teachers and students focus their efforts each week and move the group from superficial learning to the demonstration of advanced musical skills.

- Write down the three comments you heard from the podium this past week. Were the comments directed to you and your section or to the group as a whole?
- Be very specific as to what the comments were about. Were the corrections about notes, rhythms, posture, tuning, fingers, bowing, dynamics, articulation, etc.? How many times were the comments repeated?

Please note: We do not expect an exact count, but just notate if the corrections were repeated.

Next musical comments:

- Write down the three comments you heard from the podium this past week. Were the comments directed to you and your section or to the group as a whole?
- Be very specific as to what the comments were about. Were they about musical phrasing, balance, breath marks, or emotional playing; in other words, were they about what is behind the musical symbols or musical expression?

Based upon the previous comments, are there areas that you should strengthen in your playing? If you need to take responsibility for moving the group from basic corrections to a higher-level, musically oriented rehearsal, what will you do this next week in your practice?

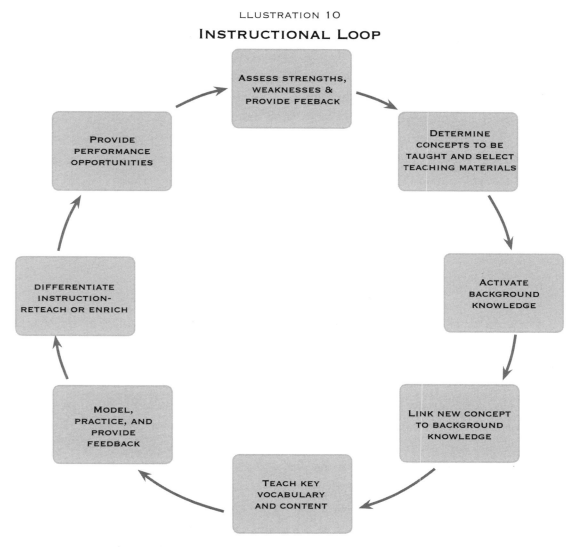

LLUSTRATION 10
INSTRUCTIONAL LOOP

The Instructional Loop illustrates how music teachers can design purposeful instruction that maximizes and elevates student learning. The loop begins when the teacher assesses student strengths and weaknesses.

INSTRUCTIONAL LOOP

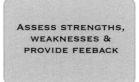

Assessing individual student and group strengths and weaknesses and providing feedback is only possible if the skills and content of the course have been clearly identified and articulated to the students. (For more information on identifying skills and designing assessments, please refer to *Scale Your Way to Music Assessment*, Chapters 2 and 3.

The teacher then provides specific feedback as to where each student is in terms of skill attainment so that he or she understands what work needs to be done regarding weaknesses, and what strengths he or she can continue to build upon. This feedback sets the purpose for the teacher and the students. In this way, teachers have set the focus for the daily rehearsals that will culminate in the performance event, and the students can develop skills as independent musicians who focus their independent practice time to maximize learning. The weekly writing and self-assessing and the continual goal setting supports not only focused development of musical skills, but also practice of the literacy skills so essential to the Common Core State Standards.

**DETERMINE CONCEPTS
TO BE TAUGHT AND
SELECT TEACHING
MATERIALS**

Once the teacher has identified which skills and content students have mastered and which skills and content they are lacking, then the teacher can determine the concepts for the unit of instruction. For the music education classroom, the unit of instruction will be considered to be the instructional time before the performance, approximately six to eight weeks. Additionally, the teacher can now select the materials, which in the case of the performance class would be the music to be learned. It is very important that the music is selected only after a careful assessment of student strengths and weaknesses. If a director selects a piece that is too difficult to be played with deep understanding during a unit, then students are only going to learn the piece at a superficial level. Moreover, if the director selects a piece that is too easy and does not challenge students to grow, then they will have a group that never moves to a higher performance level. Students who find compositions too difficult may give up if the piece cannot be played immediately; on the other hand, if the piece is easy, then some students may not reach their potential. At either level of difficulty, students may become unmotivated, discipline problems may result, and there will be a missed opportunity to develop the valuable twenty-first-century life and career skill of persistence. At the end of the day, selection of music is a critical step in the Instructional Loop.

**ACTIVATE
BACKGROUND
KNOWLEDGE**

Now that the music has been selected, the next part of the process involves the teacher activating the students' background knowledge to connect the new learning to what students already know. For example, if students have previously played a march, the director could ask students to list the different sections of the march and what they would expect to see in the march they will play today. The director could even ask a simple question, such as, "When are marches played? What time signature would you expect a march to be in? Why aren't marches in ¾ time? What happens to the key at the trio section? How is the key change at the trio related to the original key? What happens at the end of the trio? What compositional names are used for the various sections in a march? Name the sections." Rather than have the students begin at bar one without any time to prepare for learning, the concept of activating background knowledge allows the students to engage in thought and prepare for the acquisition of new knowledge and/or skills.

LINK NEW CONCEPT
TO BACKGROUND
KNOWLEDGE

So, now that the students' background knowledge has been activated, teachers should purposefully link the new knowledge to what students already know. In the case of a march, perhaps students are only familiar with patriotic American marches, but they are not familiar with ones from Spain. Or perhaps they have sung traditional hymns in church, but are not familiar with a more contemporary one that uses the traditional themes in more modern ways. Identifying the similarities between what they know and what they will learn assists students as they build their base of musical knowledge; once those similarities have formed the base of understanding, teachers can then help students link the differences and expand that base even further into the acquisition of new concepts.

TEACH KEY
VOCABULARY
AND CONTENT

Just as with the learning of new concepts, unfamiliar vocabulary should be explicitly taught. Teachers should pre-teach new vocabulary; when students come across words in the music, they already have an understanding of what they mean. Just as in the previous step where new concepts are linked to ones that are familiar, teachers should facilitate the connection of new words to ones that the students already know. This connection will provide a context for the new word and help the students be able to associate that word to something already familiar, thus making the word more memorable. The stage for learning has been set, and now is the time for teacher modeling, group rehearsal, and independent practice.

> MODEL,
> PRACTICE, AND
> PROVIDE
> FEEDBACK

During the practice stage of the Instructional Loop, it is very important for the teacher to provide specific feedback to the ensemble or students as to their progress toward the articulated learning targets. Many opportunities should be offered to students for formative assessment of skills, both individually and as a group. These formative assessments allow students to hone the skills and content knowledge necessary for the summative performance, but only if the feedback is timely and specific. Vague statements during a rehearsal or lesson, such as "You played well," although they may initially make the students feel good, don't really help the students identify why they played well, i.e., "Your tempos were consistent." Additionally, if the students' performance was weak, comments such as "Taking a breath before this phrase will allow you to reach the high note," will help the students make greater progress toward attainment of musical skills. By using appropriate musical terminology, teachers are modeling for the students the language they want students to use when they self-assess and/or peer-assess, thus strengthening and deepening the overall foundation of student musical understanding.

> DIFFERENTIATE
> INSTRUCTION-
> RETEACH OR ENRICH

Very few classrooms have students who learn at the same pace and are at the same level of skill development and understanding; therefore, teachers must embed opportunities for differentiation of instruction. These occasions to reteach when skills are lacking and to enrich when students have mastered or attained a high skill level should occur at regular intervals in the music classroom. Be it in small group ensembles purposefully designed to focus on specific skill or through assigning a solo that features a student's strengths while building weaker skills, directors should seek openings to insert chances for students to work on individual skills in addition to whole-group instruction.

PROVIDE
PERFORMANCE
OPPORTUNITIES

Finally, once students reach a level of competence in their abilities, the desire to showcase their efforts on a wider scale increases. Performance opportunities can vary from informal (playing a solo for peers in a classroom or parents at home), to formal (school or community concerts), to more high stakes, such as a state solo and ensemble or large group competition. Planning consistent occasions for students to play music that highlights their learning not only enhances student motivation, but also provides students with valuable feedback on their progress toward skill attainment.

Chapter 6
Three Steps in Creating a Musical Performance Unit

Several steps must occur before a teacher can design an effective musical performance unit.

ILLUSTRATION 11

To understand how to implement these steps to create a performance unit that incorporates the Common Core State Standards, let's examine each one separately.

PRIORITIZE KNOWLEDGE AND SKILLS TO BE LEARNED IN THE COURSE

If I walked into your classroom and asked your students what they were going to learn this year in your class, would they be able to tell me specifically what skills they were learning for each grade level in the following areas? Would they also be able to identify the skill focus for the larger ensemble?

1. Listening/aural skills
2. Written theory skills
3. Performance skills

When I have asked that question in the districts I have worked with, the students are unable to identify the specific skill focus. At first, the directors will say, "Yes, my students do know what we are working on." However, when asked about specific skills and individual documentation of what skills are valued, they will admit that their students could not answer that question, and "Neither can I." This is a key revelation. Once you realize that the students and you really don't have a set of specific skills to develop for each year in your program in the three areas of listening, written theory, and performance skills, you realize that you and your students do not have clearly defined learning targets. As a result, you are probably fixing mistakes from the podium as they arise, when in fact those mistakes were destined to happen because the students had not learned the new skill or had not taken responsibility for mastering those skills that are in the music you have selected. If you have read *Scale Your Way to Music Assessment,* Chapter 2, "Generate a List of Musical Skills,"and Chapter 3, "Align Musical Skills," in addition to *Grading for Musical Excellence,* Chapter 9, "Using Data to Create a Differentiated Grading System," you will have already begun to understand how to implement this chapter. But, if you are not familiar with those chapters, I suggest you read those books for further understanding while we give you an overview of the process.

A quality assessment program that allows teachers and students to understand where the student is starting and where the student needs to go is an inherent component of implementing the Common Core State Standards. In a nutshell, the teacher must know what needs to be taught and at what level in the classroom. Once the music educator knows that information, then selecting the music or units for the year is based upon data, not intuition, about where the students are and what the director wants them to learn. Defining the skills that are valued allows teachers to focus their energy on those skills in a variety of ways. It is not enough just to teach the skills through the rehearsal. Some of the musical skills you value may be enhanced using a combination of traditional teaching methods and a focus on key Common Core State Standards that provide musical background knowledge or key musical terminology that will provide a depth of experience for the students. Thus, students will move from basic understanding to mastery and the ability to demonstrate understanding independently or as a group in high-level assessments. Get your list of skills and look at which ones can be taught or reinforced using the Common Core English Language Arts or Mathematics Standards. I will give you some suggestions later in the book, but first let's only consider music performance classes.

Music performance classes may differ from other disciplines because the same students repeat the class or take multiple music classes within the same year. Music teachers have the rare opportunity to create a set of skills that is valued by the department, ones that students need to understand and be able to demonstrate. Student growth can be tracked through assessments and a diverse learning environment can be structured so that students at the top are challenged, whereas students at the bottom are supported. Having this information makes the music selection process more analytical and based upon student skill levels rather than random choices based on the whim of the director. The music selection process becomes more purposeful and designed to move student skills from point A to point B. In essence, it allows students to move from a basic understanding of the skills to an in-depth understanding fueled by assessments that allow students to demonstrate skills and show mastery through performance, creation, reading, or writing.

> ### DETERMINE LEVELS FOR MASTERY

This next step sets the groundwork for your assessment and feedback system to assist you in differentiating your teaching.

Determining the level of mastery of each student allows the teacher and the students to select the best method for learning and applying the skill both in and outside the classroom. Another way to think of this is that your school's teaching staff are at different levels of understanding about subjects, such as classroom management, assessment, assessment creation, parent communication, grading, and understanding of the Common Core. When the administration sets the goals for the year, they have to look at what is the current level of understanding of the goals they want to accomplish. Once they have that information, they can design workshops for the less-skilled staff and more advanced workshops for those who have greater understanding. I am sure you have been in workshops or clinic sessions that you thought were irrelevant because they were treating everyone the same regardless of the level of understanding. When this happens, the participants often become disengaged from the process. Think about that in relation to your classroom. Are you teaching everyone the same way? Focusing on the struggling students may cause the students who have mastered the skill to become disengaged; similarly, teaching to the top few students may cause students on the other end to lose focus. By having a grip on each student's level of musical understanding, the teacher can better determine the Common Core focus that will challenge the upper-level while encouraging the lower-level students. Without this information, the chance of the group reaching an in-depth level of musical understanding is limited.

> ### CREATE ASSESSMENTS THAT MEASURE VALUED KNOWLEDGE AND SKILLS

The third step is by far the most rewarding. This step of developing a series of formative and summative tests that incorporate the Common Core State Standards will enhance your ability to measure what you value and will allow you and your students to understand where they are in developing these valued skills through a variety of assessments.

The best way to think of creating an assessment is to "Value what you assess, and assess what you value." In other words, don't test what is not significant. More important, those valued skills should be measured in numerous ways or multiple periods of time. Assessment is where we can bring together performance skills, listening skills, and written theory skills through the vehicle of authentic assessments. Having the students write about skill development and growth through goal setting and weekly review of their progress (Common Core Writing Standard 1) places the responsibility for those skills squarely on the students and the teacher. First, the students must chart and reflect on individual growth through practice so that the teacher can understand student perception of progress toward goals and provide specific suggestions as to how to improve weak skills and reinforce strong skills. Sight-reading assessments provide additional opportunities for students to demonstrate performance skills through a different venue, whereas written theory tests ask students to analyze written music through multiple-choice or open-ended written questions.

By incorporating a variety of assessments into the music classroom, students must explain, demonstrate, analyze, synthesize, or create thematically, compositionally, and harmonically the skills that we value in the performance classroom in a variety of ways. Not everyone is good at writing, performing, speaking, or taking paper/pencil tests, but if students are allowed multiple avenues to demonstrate their understanding, then perhaps the teacher will have a stronger grasp about what students actually know. For example, a student might recognize intervals on a written page more easily than listening to them or performing them accurately due to the maturity needed to develop their ear. Although combining the visual with the listening is an important component of developing this understanding, as the teacher, I need to provide multiple opportunities for the students to develop those skills in a variety of scenarios. Thus, both teacher and students are focusing their efforts on a common goal that would affect the music selection and the skills that are taught. Why would music with very difficult intervals be selected when the majority of students in the group can't differentiate between simple thirds and fourths? Not taking intervals into account could cause the music teacher to spend an inordinate amount of time correcting the mistakes in intervals rather than "getting to the music." Don't set yourself and your students up for failure by selecting music that is way beyond their skill level. Music selection should be based upon the skill level of the individual students and the group. In a later chapter, you will see some examples of how to implement Common Core ideas in combination with written, listening, and performance assessments to pre-teach skills in a musical selection.

CHAPTER 7
SIX STEPS IN HOW TO DESIGN A UNIT
FOR A MUSICAL PERFORMANCE

Once the knowledge and skills have been determined, the levels of mastery set, and the assessments created for the overall course, the teacher can begin to design individual units for a musical performance class. The following six steps set the stage for an effectively designed unit. Several of the steps are also part of the Instructional Loop that focuses on the broader picture of the overall course; the steps in this phase of unit design, however, spotlight the specific skill focus and concentrate efforts on developing this skill during the particular unit or concert performance event.

ILLUSTRATION 12

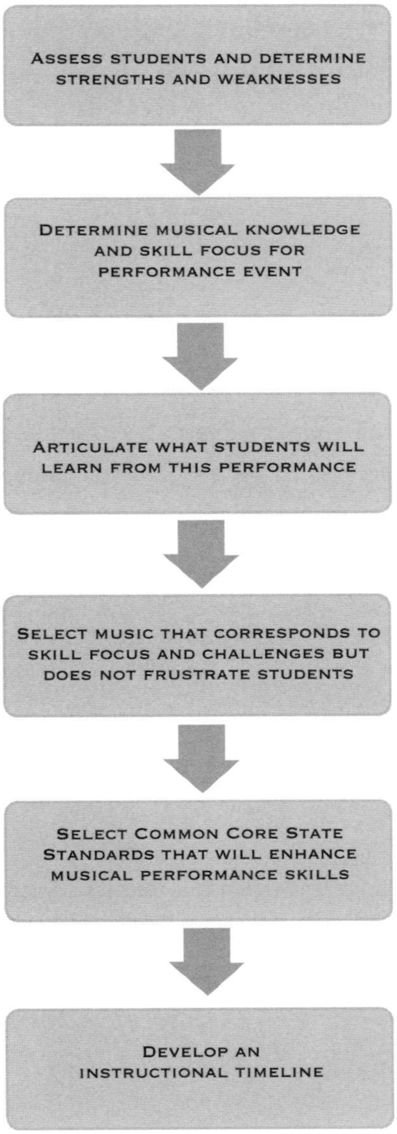

ASSESS STUDENTS AND DETERMINE STRENGTHS AND WEAKNESSES

DETERMINE MUSICAL KNOWLEDGE AND SKILL FOCUS FOR PERFORMANCE EVENT

ARTICULATE WHAT STUDENTS WILL LEARN FROM THIS PERFORMANCE

SELECT MUSIC THAT CORRESPONDS TO SKILL FOCUS AND CHALLENGES BUT DOES NOT FRUSTRATE STUDENTS

SELECT COMMON CORE STATE STANDARDS THAT WILL ENHANCE MUSICAL PERFORMANCE SKILLS

DEVELOP AN INSTRUCTIONAL TIMELINE

Let's look at each step more closely and how to implement and understand the steps in relation to each other.

> **ASSESS STUDENTS AND DETERMINE STRENGTHS AND WEAKNESSES**

First, the teacher must know the strengths and weaknesses of the students, and thus, the ensemble. Does the group understand basic rhythmic structures and are they ready to move onto ones that are more complex? Is the range greater for one section over another? Is intonation accuracy stronger in the woodwinds, while the brass need work in that area? Do the altos have trouble reading the notes on the staff and hearing pitch when they move toward the upper end of the range? Teachers must not only assess the playing or singing performance skills of the students individually, but also the students' knowledge of musical content. For example, what musical vocabulary or history do the students understand; what will need to be taught in order for students to move to a higher level of understanding?

> **DETERMINE MUSICAL KNOWLEDGE AND SKILL FOCUS FOR PERFORMANCE EVENT**

Once teachers have a grasp as to what the students know and can do, and what their strengths and weaknesses are, they can move on to step 2 and decide the content knowledge and skill focus for the specific performance event. This content and skill focus will guide the remainder of the steps in designing the performance unit. Now that the content and skill focus has been determined and clearly articulated, music can be selected for the performance event.

> **ARTICULATE WHAT STUDENTS WILL LEARN FROM THIS PERFORMANCE**

The third step, articulate what students will learn from the performance event, would not be possible without a clear focus. The music director must be able to say, "From the Winter Concert, I want my students to know _____ and be able to do _____." Then that statement must be shared with the students so that the entire group knows the focus for the rehearsals and the concert. Posting these learning targets in the classroom will also demonstrate to the students the level of commitment the director has made in helping all students reach the level of mastery needed for a successful performance.

> SELECT MUSIC THAT CORRESPONDS TO
> SKILL FOCUS AND CHALLENGES BUT
> DOES NOT FRUSTRATE STUDENTS

The fourth step regarding music selection should be based upon individual student, section, and group strengths and weaknesses. Care must be taken to select music that will move students forward toward growth in the areas of focus. The music must also be complex enough to challenge students, but not so difficult that they become frustrated. Because few groups have students at one level of ability, when it comes to developing the instructional timeline, the teacher will most likely want to consider ways to differentiate instruction to address that variety of skill levels. A discussion of differentiation strategies will follow in a later chapter.

> SELECT COMMON CORE STATE
> STANDARDS THAT WILL ENHANCE
> MUSICAL PERFORMANCE SKILLS

The fifth step begins after the music has been selected. The director can now determine which Common Core State Standards will enhance student musical knowledge and skills. For example, having students at the end of a rehearsal write about their individual contribution toward reaching one of the performance unit's skill focus would address Writing Standard 1 where students must support an opinion, or claim, with evidence. Or if a skill focus for the performance event were to increase the level of balance and blend in an ensemble, then the twenty-first-century skill of collaboration would enhance the group and individual effort toward achieving that goal. The intent of blending the Common Core into your classroom is to enhance learning in the musical classroom. Spending time on these activities may at first take time, but it is time well spent, and time that will save time in the long run.

> DEVELOP AN
> INSTRUCTIONAL TIMELINE

The sixth and final step in the process is to design an instructional timeline that will guide instruction in the classroom on a daily basis, from the time the pieces are introduced to when they are performed. This timeline is not meant to be an irrevocable document; rather, it is a guide that is meant to be flexible and fluid, one that will change as the teachers adapt their instruction to the needs of the students. Initially, the importance of developing this timeline is to guide pacing; the teacher must consciously plan instruction logically and sequentially, realistically determining the approximate time it takes for students to master the concepts, content, and skills demanded by the materials. Anticipating the time it takes to teach certain skills or elements will ensure that key skills are taught, that time is not spent on skills that are not a priority, and that by the end of the unit (i.e., the performance), adequate time is devoted to the skills necessary to a quality performance. It also allows music teachers to strategically embed Common Core State Standards into the curriculum that will support the development of musical skills over time.

Illustration 13 is a sample Instructional Timeline for a performance. Note that when designing a timeline, the teacher should consider time spent in class as well as the time outside of class that can be used to enhance student learning.

Note that the Instructional Timeline references "focused rehearsal" and "focused independent practice." The term "focused" in these instances means that the skill selected as the goal for the unit or performance event is attended to during rehearsals and independent practice. Although the director will work on other skills as needed during the rehearsals, the director should make a conscious effort to ensure that some part of the rehearsal is dedicated to working on the skill for the unit. Likewise, students should plan their practice sessions around the skill that has been determined as the area of focus. If rehearsals and practices have a clear focus, then progress toward mastery of goals for the group and the individual will be achieved.

Now that a performance unit has been effectively designed around a specific skill set, and teacher and student efforts are concentrated on developing this skill, we can move on to discussing strategies that directors can embed in their rehearsals that will enhance music performance skills.

ILLUSTRATION 13
INSTRUCTIONAL TIMELINE FOR A PERFORMANCE

In Class

Introduce piece by activating background knowledge and pre-teaching key vocabulary and musical concepts

Focused rehearsal

Read short synopsis of piece/composer. Have students provide evidence from piece that links piece to this information.

Focused rehearsal

Formatively assess and provide feedback to students on musical skills and knowledge

Focused rehearsal

Performance

Written reflection on individual and group performance

Outside Class

Students reflect on assessment stengths & weaknesses and set goals for unit

Focused independent practice

Focused independent practice

Student reflection about progress and goal adjustment if necessary independent practice

Individually perform for teacher and receive feedback to refocus independent practice.

Focused independent practice

Performance

Written reflection on individual and group performance

CHAPTER 8
FLUENCY IN THE MUSIC CLASSROOM

WHAT IS FLUENCY AND HOW DOES IT BUILD MUSICAL SKILLS?

Fluency is the ability to do something easily or smoothly, to have command over the skills necessary to perform a task. When students are fluent in their skills, there is an automaticity that occurs. When students learn to read and become fluent, they no longer hesitate or pause on individual words, reading in a halting manner. It is as if one can hear the individual neurons in the brain sputtering, trying to make connections between sounds and words. On the other hand, students who are fluent are able to read with expression, paying attention to punctuation. Additionally, fluency is directly related to the complexity of the text. Readers who are fluent at reading sixth-grade level texts may stumble when asked to read text at the tenth-grade level.

But, fluency is a complex skill. Some students who can read fluently may not have the accompanying comprehension skills. These students, "word callers," understand the sound/symbol relationships and the rules of punctuation but may have difficulty with the underlying meaning of the text. Thus, when the text complexity is ramped up, they fall behind because the skill of inferential reading becomes more of the focus.

Fluency in musical skills is closely related to fluency in reading. As with reading, students need to read music fluently, making connections between the notes on the page and the fingerings or pitches on the instrument or voice. Without musical fluency, students will be unable to reach a higher level of performance by playing "beyond" the notes with musical expression. Once students become fluent in their musical skills, they are able to pay attention to the nuances of the musical symbols, such as breath marks, slurs, tonguing, phrase marking, and articulation. These elements, if comprehended by the students, allow the students to play or sing the music with an enhanced interpretation of the piece. Just as an author uses connotations of words and punctuation to add meaning to a text, the composer adds musical symbols to communicate meaning. Hence, students are unable to get to the meaning of the piece without the underlying ability to play or sing fluently. If a majority of the musicians in an ensemble have a low level of fluency, the level of the overall group will be affected and the musical experience will be minimal.

Similar to reading, musical fluency is also related to the complexity of the composition. Students may be able to read a Grade 1 or 2 piece of music with ease, but fluency suffers when the piece becomes more complicated. So, how can music educators strengthen fluency in their students? Fluency strategies used in reading may provide a key to building fluency skills in musicians.

Common Core State Standards for Reading emphasize fluency, particularly in Standard 1 (Read closely to determine what the text says explicitly and to make logical inferences from it); Standard 2 (Determine central ideas or themes); and Standard 10 (Read and comprehend complex texts independently and proficiently). By replacing the word "read" with "play or sing" and the word "text" with "composition", one can see the strong relationship between reading and musical performance.

FLUENCY STRATEGIES THAT BUILD MUSICAL UNDERSTANDING AND PERFORMANCE SKILLS

Strategies that are used to build fluency in reading may also prove beneficial in the music classroom. The following fluency strategies could be used to enhance a student's musical performance.

CHORAL READING – CHORAL PLAYING/SINGING

Playing or singing in unison is one way to build fluency skills. Reading teachers use this strategy when they have students read the same text together aloud. By reading alongside other students, students must keep up the pace with their peers. Also, choral playing/singing compels students to play in tempo and gain confidence as they benefit from hearing one another's interpretation of the music. Starting slowly at first, but keeping the pace rhythmically accurate, and then gradually increasing the tempo will assist students in developing fluency. Variations on choral playing/singing can be used with scales in which the group can play the first time and individuals can play the second time. Additionally, it benefits the group to be able to play the melody so that each musician in the ensemble has an understanding of the importance of the melody and to connect their part to support the major theme of the piece.

REPEATED READING – REPEATED PLAYING OR SINGING

Reading a text more than once also builds fluency skills. Students can work on fluency when they are not worried about the words, and in music's case, the notes. Speaking the text in a choral piece repeatedly before adding the music allows students to then focus on the notes rather than the written text. Many times the text of a composition is written in a language unfamiliar to students; thus, repeated reading of the text alone is an important strategy to help create fluency when students sing the piece.

READING LESS-COMPLEX TEXT OR COMPOSITIONS

Fluency breaks down when the demands of the text or music increase. Therefore, playing or singing compositions that are within the students' independent level of playing will help the students build skills in fluency.

READING HIGH-INTEREST, FAMILIAR TEXTS OR COMPOSITIONS

Students who have background knowledge of a particular subject or tend to be interested in a topic are able to comprehend a higher level of text difficulty. Similarly, building skills in fluency will be easier if students have knowledge of the type or style of music, an affinity for learning about that style of music, or have heard the music in another setting. Using these types of compositions will help students gain fluency that can then be transferred to unknown pieces.

FOCUS ON HIGH-FREQUENCY WORDS OR NOTE PATTERNS

Providing students with opportunities to learn high-frequency patterns—be they words in a text or notes in music—can also develop skills in fluency. Building automaticity in fingerings by having students play or sing scales from the pieces they will be performing will provide a foundation of skills. Additionally, development of automaticity in high frequency rhythm patterns will pay dividends down the road. Pre-teaching musical skills that will build fluency in the pieces to be performed should be an important component of a musical rehearsal. All in all, spending time on fluency in the music classroom will build the skills necessary to reach high levels of musical performance.

CHAPTER 9
WRITING IN THE MUSIC CLASSROOM

HOW DOES WRITING ELEVATE MUSICAL SKILLS AND KNOWLEDGE?

Writing in the music classroom compels students to articulate an understanding of musical vocabulary, skills, and concepts. Writing moves students to higher levels and deeper understanding when they are asked to explain, describe, analyze, evaluate, and create. If students don't write in the classroom, how does a teacher truly know the level of their understanding? Asking students to play cannot be the sole demonstration of the depth or level of understanding of complex musical concepts. When students write, the teacher is given a window into the brain, thus allowing misconceptions to be corrected and superficial understanding to be addressed. Whether it is to defend an opinion, to explain the steps in a process, or to supply a solution to a problem, writing gives teachers an authentic view of how a student thinks.

MAKE TIME TO WRITE AND SAVE REHEARSAL TIME

Although it may seem that writing in the music classroom is taking away time from the rehearsal, in the end, time spent on having students write saves rehearsal time because students retain the information and really understand it. Granted, teachers will have to read what the students write, which adds time to an already busy schedule; in the long run, however, having students write consistently in the music classroom will pay off in deeper understanding and students who truly understand the concepts and skills required by the music they are performing.

Teachers will also find that they have to repeat themselves less, always correcting the same mistakes. As a formative assessment, writing changes a teacher's instruction since it allows teachers to know what their students know, and thus, they are able to adjust their instruction to meet their students' needs.

WRITING STRATEGIES TO BUILD MUSICAL UNDERSTANDING AND PERFORMANCE SKILLS

The following writing strategies are ones that music educators can use to embed writing in their classrooms. These strategies will build the base of literacy skills and support the school-wide focus on the Common Core State Standards. Providing students with a template or graphic organizer will ensure that students can clearly identify the purpose of their writing because these organizers are based on the specific text structure of the writing students are asked to do. The Common Core State Standards specifically address argumentative writing (Writing Standard 1) and informational/explanatory writing (Writing Standard 2). Furthermore, the Common Core focus is about writing that is coherent and organized (Writing Standard 4) and that students plan and revise their writing (Writing Standard 5). Many of the writing standards can be addressed through the use of graphic organizers that help students understand how a structure enhances writing and serves as an organizational aide in the writing process. Additionally, organizers connect writing across the curriculum, since other disciplines use similar templates to help their students organize their writing.

Expository writing in the classroom usually falls into one of six basic structures: description, sequence, comparison/contrast, problem/solution, cause/effect, and argumentative. The first five types of writing are addressed by Common Core State Standard – Writing 2, and argumentative writing is covered in Writing Standard 1. Accompanying each structure are suggested usages for writing in the music classroom.

DESCRIPTION

Descriptive writing can be used when teachers want students to investigate a musical topic or concept. Students might research, for example, a composer or a musical genre, such as the blues, marches, or spirituals. When students are asked to dig deeper into the background of a genre or composer, they are better able to understand the context for their performance, and thus, their musical performance is enhanced. Performing without deeper musical understanding is akin to what reading experts refer to as "word calling." Some students may be able to pronounce words well because they understand the basic rules of phonics and are able to memorize words that do not fit the phonemic patterns. As the text grows in complexity, however, these students are unable to understand the deeper, or inferential, meanings embedded in the text. As a result, they are unable to read with expression and infer meaning because to them, reading is just pronouncing or "calling" the words. Moreover, in music, some students may just "play notes," rather than play with musical expressiveness. Getting them to dig more deeply into the context of the music through investigation of genres, theory, techniques, and composers will allow students to have the background knowledge to give meaning to the notes. See Illustration 14 for a graphic organizer that assists students in writing a descriptive essay.

SEQUENCE

Music is a skill, and thus, students often have to understand the sequence of steps in a particular process, for example, a warm-up or putting a reed on a woodwind instrument. Having students write the steps of a process is often eye opening for the teacher. So often, we assume that students "know" the process because they at least follow along with the group. Having students articulate a process can be enlightening because it brings to light individual misconceptions that may be lurking under the surface of a rehearsal. Addressing and correcting these misconceptions that may not be discovered in a group setting certainly will have a positive impact on their performance. Please see Illustration 15 for a graphic organizer that assists students in writing the steps in a sequence.

COMPARISON AND CONTRAST

In a meta-analysis of learning strategies, Robert Marzano observes that having students identify similarities and differences is a strategy with high leverage. In other words, this strategy produces positive learning results in classrooms when it is used as an integral part of instructional practice. The classic organizer for comparing and contrasting is, of course, the Venn diagram. What may be missing on many Venn diagrams, however, is a space for students to summarize their findings of similarities and differences. Having students write this final "conclusion" is important because it requires students to synthesize the information they have learned, a higher-level thinking skill. Please see Illustration 16 for an example of a comparison/contrast graphic organizer. Assignments that ask students to compare and contrast various musical techniques or genres lead to a higher level of understanding. Another suggestion would be for students to compare and contrast their part in the music with another part. For example, how does my soprano part fit in with the bass or alto lines? How does my viola part relate to the cello or violin lines? How do I relate to my section in a positive manner? Developing an understanding of how an individual part relates to the ensemble is crucial in creating balance and blend in a group, and having students articulate their role can give teachers insight into how students individually perceive their musical role.

PROBLEM/SOLUTION

The problem-solution text structure can be more complex, especially if the problem is complex and not entirely solved by a single solution. This type of writing can be very motivating, however, because students enjoy solving problems and giving their input regarding which solution is the best fit. The problems can range from individual difficulties that a student may have (i.e., "I am unable to sing or play high notes") to group-generated issues (such as, "Our marching band needs to improve its marching and maneuvering"). With individual problems, students can seek out expert advice concerning various ways to extend their range, which adds to the depth of their musical content knowledge and certainly improves their performance. Please see Illustration 17 for a graphic organizer that assists students in writing a problem-solution essay.

CAUSE/EFFECT

Another structure that prompts students to higher levels of thought is being able to articulate the relationship between cause and effect. Understanding this concept helps students associate actions with results. A sample cause-and-effect writing prompt might ask students to describe the relationship of posture to tone quality. If I slump in my chair, what happens to my tone? If I sit up with my feet firmly on the floor, holding my instrument correctly, how does that change affect the quality of my tone? Helping students to identify the effect that follows a cause is essential if students are to take responsibility and, by extension, ownership in making progress toward their goals. Please see Illustration 18 for a graphic organizer that addresses cause and effect writing.

ARGUMENT

Finally, students should be able to argue a point by offering conceptual support for their opinions, Common Core State Standard – Writing 1. After a concert, students could be asked to identify their own musical strengths and weaknesses (claim), and then provide evidence. To fully defend a claim, students will have to demonstrate an understanding of music vocabulary, concepts, and skills. Depending upon the maturity of the students, a teacher may provide a word bank of expected terms to include in the writing. Through the analysis of their own performance, students will be able to evaluate where they are currently in their performance skills and determine where they want to go next. This self-assessment creates ownership and reinforces the connection of effort and practice with outcomes. For an example of an argument graphic organizer, please see Illustration 19.

ILLUSTRATION 14

DESCRIPTION

Name:_____   Date:_____

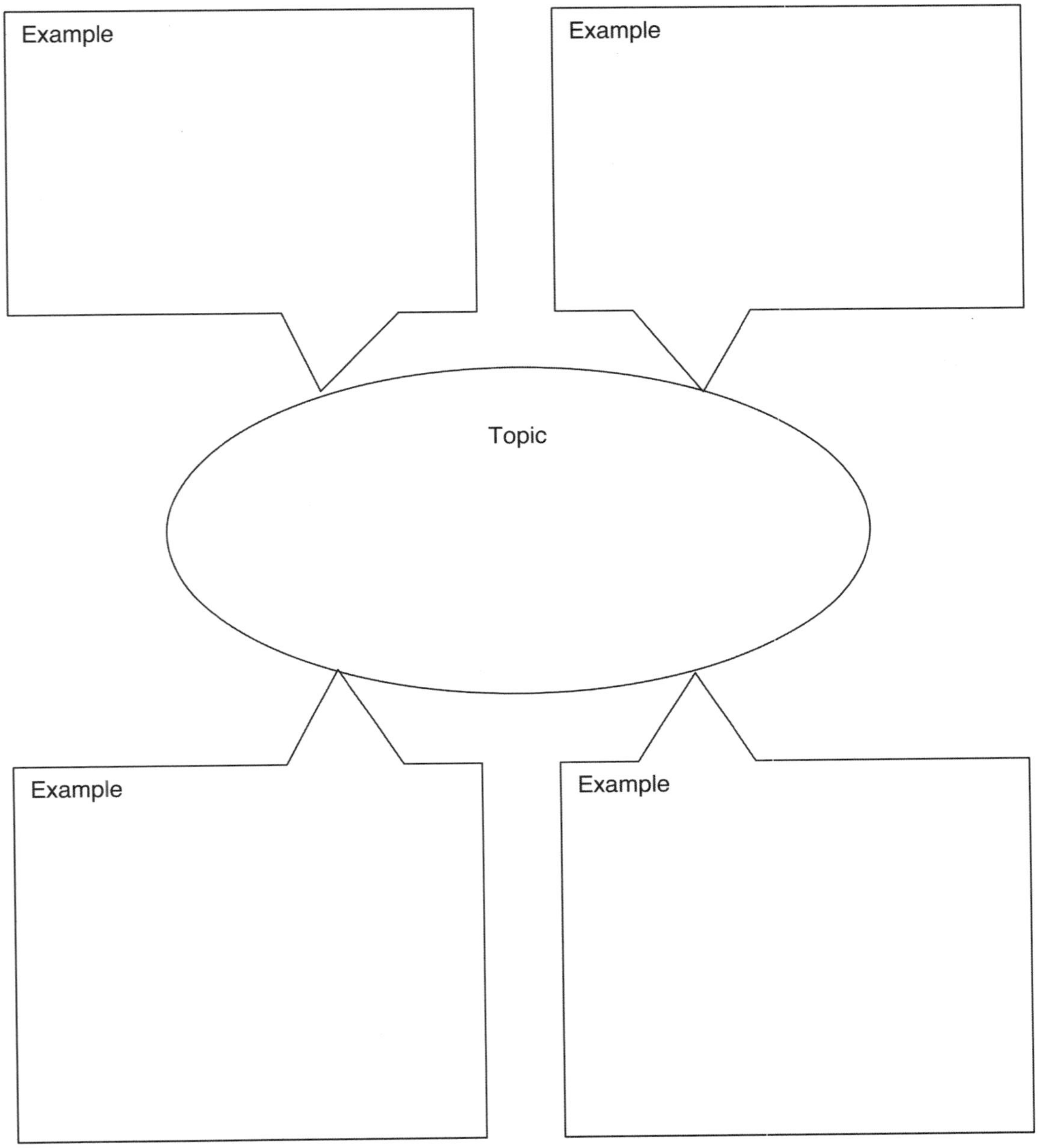

Example	Example

Topic

Example	Example

ILLUSTRATION 15

SEQUENCE

Name:_____   Date:_____

Step 1

Step 2

Step 3

Step 4

Step 5

ILLUSTRATION 16

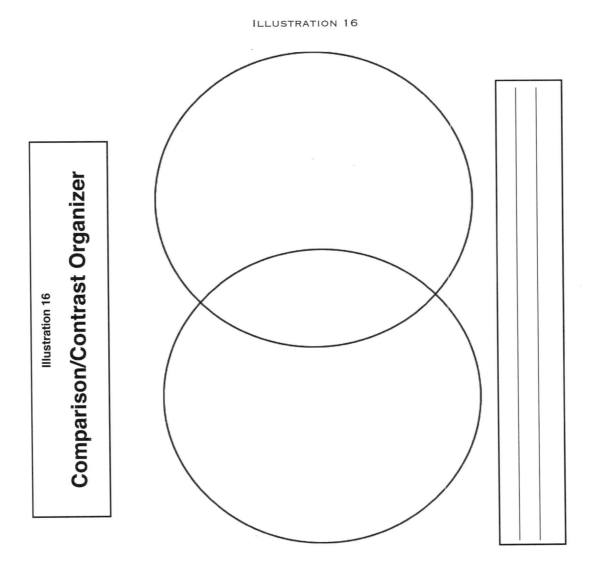

Illustration 16

Comparison/Contrast Organizer

ILLUSTRATION 17
PROBLEM - SOLUTION

Name:_____ Date:_____

Problem or Conflict

Possible Solution	Possible Solution	Possible Solution
Pros	Pros	Pros
Cons	Cons	Cons

Final Solution

ILLUSTRATION 18

CAUSE - EFFECT

Name:_____   Date:_____

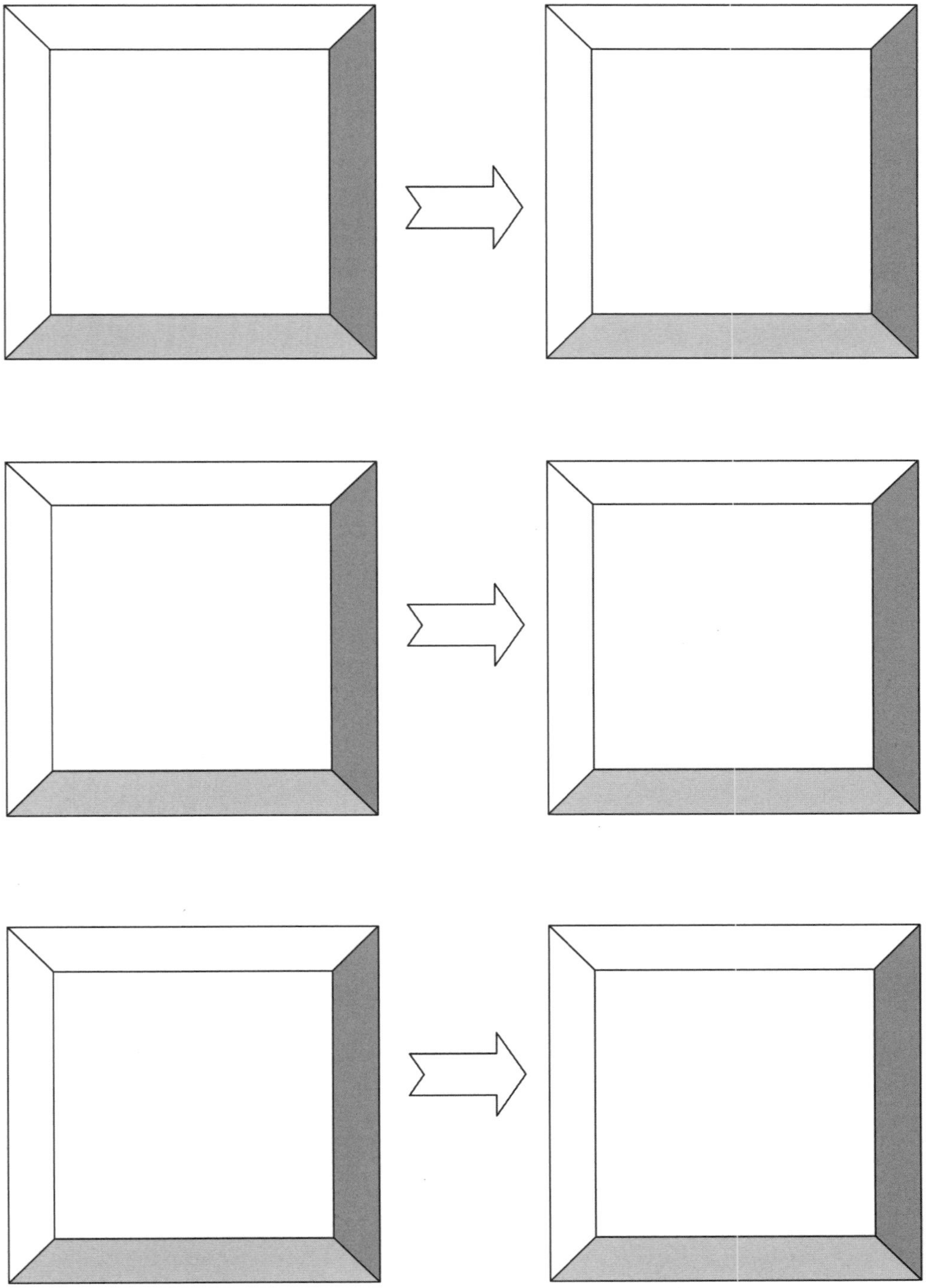

ILLUSTRATION 19

OPINION-PROOF/ARGUMENTATIVE WRITING

Name:_____   Date:_____

Topic: What issue do you want to address?

What is your opinion about the issue?

What is your evidence?

List two supporting facts

1.

2.

What is your evidence?

List two supporting facts

1.

2.

Conclusion: What would you like the person to do?

PROVIDING FEEDBACK TO STUDENTS ON THEIR WRITING

Providing feedback to students concerning their writing may feel uncomfortable for music teachers. They also may be the recipients of comments from students, such as, "This is music class, not English. Why do I have to write?" Ever the more important for music teachers to communicate clearly to their students that writing is a necessary skill and form of communication in all disciplines! So, what is the best way to provide feedback to students so they can be more effective communicators of our subject area?

TEACHER/STUDENT

In their research, Hattie and Timperley (2007) described four types of feedback: (1) Feedback about the task; in other words, did students complete the written assignment as asked? Did they provide a claim and then support that claim with conceptual evidence? How solid is their claim and is the evidence sufficient and logical? (2) Feedback about the process; in a music class, this feedback can be used in response to student reflections on their progress toward goals. For example, if a student has set a goal about improving their high range, the teacher can provide specific feedback or make suggestions about exercises to improve breath support. (3) Feedback about self-regulation; this feedback concerns the learning process. General feedback such as "You did a good job!" is not helpful if it doesn't help a student to identify exactly what it was that was good. Better written feedback would be, "Your consistent practice time has helped you to play a two-octave chromatic scale." (4) Feedback about the self as a person; this feedback generally supports the achievement mindset of learning, that music is a fixed talent that is not affected by practice and effort. Overall, the most effective feedback is feedback about the process or self-regulation, because this feedback reinforces mastery learning by the student.

As far as grammar and spelling are concerned, I would not be too worried about corrections unless communication is affected, especially if the writing is done in class. As for more formal, researched papers, a separate critique for conventions of spelling, punctuation, or grammar can be used, especially if the school has a building-wide rubric for writing; however, the main goal should be to provide honest, timely feedback about the musical skill or concept that is the focus rather than getting mired down in the minutia of commenting on the mechanics of writing.

Collaboration with the English Department or language arts teachers is also recommended. They will be able to share rubrics and writing strategies that can be readily applied in the music classroom. Students will be familiar with these approaches to writing, thus allowing music teachers to concentrate on the musical content and support of the writing skills they learn in their English classes. This partnership is a win-win for all subject areas. Not only will the language arts teachers appreciate help in improving student writing across the school, but also music teachers will be seen as valued team members who provide a consistency in a school-wide approach to writing. Overall, students are the big beneficiaries as they develop focused and organized writing skills in all of their classes.

STUDENT/STUDENT

Having students provide peer feedback can also be effective. Students should use a rubric that clearly articulates the learning targets of the assignment. Additionally, peers should use proper musical terminology when providing feedback, thus reinforcing their own skills in identifying musical strengths and weaknesses.

OUTSIDE FEEDBACK

Bringing in outside sources is also valuable for students. Feedback from judges and clinicians can be analyzed to improve student performance. Using outside experts to provide written feedback also reinforces the importance of solid communication skills in the music profession.

ONLINE RESOURCES

Many software, online solutions are available to make writing not only more appealing to students, but also easier for the teacher to manage and to provide immediate feedback. For example, Google has many free applications that allow students to respond electronically to teachers. Footnotes and bibliographies can be formatted easily, using such tools as Noodle Tools. Check with your school's language arts teachers to see what software or free online resources they use. If these resources are being used widely in your building, chances are that students are already familiar with them, and they can easily be incorporated into the music classroom.

CHAPTER 10
VOCABULARY IN THE MUSIC CLASSROOM

The Common Core State Standards have a Language Anchor Standard devoted to vocabulary acquisition, Language Standard 4. Comprehension of any language, be it English, music, or mathematics is limited if one does not have a command of the vocabulary of that discipline.

WHAT VOCABULARY DO MUSICIANS NEED?

In order to answer this question, let's examine a different discipline, the Cessna private pilot training program, and how vocabulary is selected and taught. I have chosen this program because it is not taught in a K-12 system; instead, it is a real-world application. When I earned my private pilot certificate on the weekends while teaching music full time in a high school, it was one of my most eye-opening experiences that influenced my teaching and understanding of how students learn, remember, and apply what they have learned. It is well documented in educational research that students who are fully engaged in learning that is connected to them in meaningful and relevant ways retain the information much longer. The pilot training is not organized with eight weeks of classroom, followed by application of the information. Rather, the program is based upon the student learning one specific aspect of flying, followed by a rigorous written test and then application by having the student pilots test their skills in an actual airplane. The student must demonstrate understanding by performing the skill and, as a result, being held accountable for mastery of the skill. For example, one skill was learning how to taxi an airplane on the ground. The students learn only the vocabulary for that particular skill, such as rudder, toe brake, crosswind, throttle, and aileron, and thus they are focused on only one aspect of the plane. The technical terms must be applied immediately, and the students must show that they are able to perform the skill taught by taxiing the plane around on the ground while verbalizing the correct terminology.

Now let's fast forward to the music classroom. How often does a director say in rehearsal, "Do you see the dynamic marking? What does *PP* mean? Let's do it again, and use the dynamics." Do co-pilots or captains of a plane have the option to say, "Let's do it again?" Would you want to ride in the back of that plane? We want our students to understand and demonstrate the vocabulary that is needed for a particular selection automatically, interpreting the technical terms in a musically appropriate way. The lesson to be learned from the pilot training is straightforward: *Always connect music vocabulary immediately to the actual music students will perform.* Continually reinforce the idea of learning by holding students accountable for demonstrating their understanding of the terms through performance and articulation, be it by speaking or writing. Even during sight-reading, the terms in the composition should be pre-taught before playing the piece. This pre-teaching includes not only the musical terms, but also the articulations, symbols, and alternate fingerings that lend meaning to the piece. If you pre-teach the vocabulary and apply it on scales that match the key of the sight-reading piece or through chorales in the same key and hold the students responsible for demonstrating, the students will have a better chance of internalizing the meaning, rather than memorizing a few terms that will be retained for the short term and quickly forgotten by the end of the year. Answer this question below.

What comments do you repeat when your group is sight-reading? Do the students on the first reading demonstrate the behavior called for regarding the vocabulary and symbols?

_____

_____

_____

_____

_____

_____

_____

How do you know whether your students understand the vocabulary?

_____

_____

_____

Assessing key vocabulary terms before playing or singing a piece of music is key because it allows the director to focus on terms students do not understand. Pre-teaching this unfamiliar vocabulary will significantly improve the group's musical performance by allowing them to play with deeper musical understanding. You may be surprised at what your students know and what they do not know. The only way to know for sure is to conduct a pre-assessment of their vocabulary knowledge, and then to pre-teach those words or symbols. This pre-teaching will save time in the long run because students have an increased sense of purpose (i.e., when I see the word *decrescendo,* I will gradually play or sing softer), and thus they will be able to perform with greater musical understanding.

MUSIC VOCABULARY KNOWLEDGE RATING SCALE

One method of assessing student understanding of vocabulary is to have them complete a Music Vocabulary Knowledge Rating Scale. On page 87 is a blank, blackline master that asks students to respond to terms or symbols before they play a piece of music. If students say they understand a term, they must demonstrate that understanding by articulating a definition. Having this information before sight-reading a selection allows the director to determine student strengths and weaknesses, thus filling in gaps in understanding and not wasting time by teaching information that students already know.

When I first started teaching, my father, a music educator for thirty-five years, gave me this advice: "If your band can't play straight through a new piece without stopping, then the piece is too hard." At that time in music education, terms such as graphic organizers and Common Core were not words that were used. That didn't mean that these teachers didn't understand the value of pre-teaching vocabulary or making sure that they knew the students' weaknesses and strengths; rather, it meant that without an understanding of the vocabulary and the music symbols and rhythms being used in the new piece, the students would not be able to play and interpret the symbols with any degree of success. I have used my father's advice throughout my career and still find it applies in today's classrooms.

Mentally answer "yes" or "no" to questions one through six, if applicable, depending upon the type of ensemble. On questions seven through nine, write down your answers. Consider your reasons without placing the blame on yourself or others.

When your group last sight-read a piece, what were the reasons for stopping?

1. Were the rhythms new or unfamiliar?
2. Was the individual musical range more than the group could play?
3. Was the key unfamiliar?
4. Were the parts exposed, thus putting a soloist on the spot?
5. Were the second and third parts independent of the first part?
6. Did the woodwind parts require runs and finger patterns that used alternate fingerings?
7. Were the comments or mistakes you corrected because the students were unfamiliar with the musical term or had not mastered the skill in order to be able to play the symbol or term correctly?
8. What has happened in the past when the students could not play through a piece? Did they not like it, was your rehearsal tense, and did you not play the piece again?
9. What were your feelings during and after the sight-reading?
10. Did you identify any other issues that may have impacted your group's ability to sight-read a piece?

Now that you have answered the above questions, let's look more closely at the Music Vocabulary Knowledge Rating Scale that is featured in Illustration 20. You will notice five columns. The first column on the left is where you will go through your score before sight-reading the new selection and enter every term, rhythm, key, and articulation. List every term or symbol that appears on your score that students will be asked to demonstrate and then mark down the measure or page on which it appears. Hand this Rating Scale out with the music, but do not plan on playing the piece that day. Give the students, depending on the length of the piece, about ten minutes to complete the sheet and hand it back to you. Have the students mark their level of understanding in one of the three boxes to the right (No Clue)—(Seen or Heard)—(Can Define or Demonstrate the Term). When they are done, collect the sheets, and when time permits, tally up the answers on a blank form. For any area that has half or more of the students answering "No Clue" or "Seen or Heard," you should pre-teach that skill or term before sight-reading the selection. This information allows you to perceive what your students understand and what you need to teach. If half of a group does not understand the technical terms or symbols needed to play a new selection, the result is going to be less than positive, setting the stage for student and teacher frustration. Why would you put yourself and your students in a losing situation? Can you think of a coach, a manager of a business, or a military commander, just to name a few, who do not want to maximize what the people under them know and use that to their advantage? What they don't know, they teach so that they can perform the task successfully.

Think of sight-reading similar to an exercise in solving a problem, where each problem or piece has a different solution. The players are asked to respond, evaluate, and execute quickly, with very little time to think. They must react and adjust to the next situation or musical task. The Common Core State Standards demand that students be able to solve complex tasks in real time. And, the Standards require students to take the complex information from a variety of sources and use it to analyze and solve problems. That type of problem solving is what sight-reading is all about. If we, as music educators, link sight-reading with supporting the higher-level skills demanded in the twenty-first century, then we will not only enhance our value to other disciplines, but also the students will be more motivated to learn these skills that can be readily transferred to real-life situations. All in all, pre-teaching musical terms and symbols will lead to less repetition on the part of the director and greater student understanding of the music and what it takes to perform music on a high level.

ILLUSTRATION 20

Music Vocabulary Knowledge Rating Sheet

Name_____

Word/Rhythm	Page/Measure #	No Clue	Seen or Heard	Can Define and Demonstrate Symbol

DEMONSTRATING UNDERSTANDING THROUGH WRITING OR SPEAKING

Now that you have tallied up the strengths and weaknesses of your students regarding vocabulary, it is time to pre-teach the skills that are weak and reinforce the acquired skills. If you see rhythms they don't understand, then write them on the board, count them out with the students, and play familiar scales that allow the students to concentrate on the rhythms not the notes. It is assumed that you have taught your students a consistent use of musical terms and a consistent way of counting. This system should be the same one used across the entire department and by all the staff, including private teachers. Consistency in usage allows the students to move from band to orchestra to choir and hear the same terms, methods of counting, and classroom expectations. Continuity builds competence.

Here are a few more examples. If the brass instruments are required to execute double or triple tonguing in the new sight-reading, then teach them those skills in warm-up. Brass players should say the syllables first, which can be done as the band plays their scales. They say the Tu-ku or Ta-ka sounds on eighth notes while the band plays the scale in eighth notes. Similarly, the idea would be used on triple tonguing Tata-ka or Tutu-ku. Keep in mind the phrase, "You can't play it, if you can't say it." Additionally, pre-teach the keys or scales before the piece is played, stressing that students are able to identify the key as major or minor, and if it is minor, which key. I see more students failing to play a piece correctly that is in minor because no one taught them that in harmonic minor, the seventh note will be raised. The students play the major key signature in spite of what the accidentals are suggesting. Since they don't understand that concept, they make the same mistake over and over, causing the conductor to repeat corrections.

Pre-teaching activities can be fun and interesting. Consider that teaching keys will enhance your students' understanding of musical structure. Ask them to provide examples of minor and major songs. The genre itself, be it popular or classical, is not as important as the connection students are making to the harmonic structure. Additional activities that support student understanding would be to have them expand their knowledge of musical vocabulary and terms by having them write a short compare-and-contrast essay or complete a graphic organizer about the differences between major and minor keys. Use writing to further challenge the students to look more closely at the music they play, to see the patterns in the structure, all of which will foster deeper musical performances.

Demonstrating through Performance

Once you think you have taught the new term or symbol, have students demonstrate their understanding on simple scales or rhythms individually or in a group setting. Furthermore, if you had them write about a certain aspect of the music, have them listen to a similar selection and write about what they heard. You could even play a major and a minor selection and have them compare and contrast to measure their understanding. What you are doing is teaching deeper understanding in different ways. Music educators can then see that having our students understand and demonstrate musical skills in a variety of ways will strengthen their base of musical knowledge.

By now, you may be thinking, when do we get to the sight-reading we handed out? The pre-teaching should not take more than a day or two during your warm-ups. If you have to teach so much new material, then the piece is way past your group's current musical understanding, and you might need to hold off playing or sight-reading that selection until later in the year. Do you remember earlier in the book when I asked you why you select the pieces for your group, and are the compositions cultivating the skills you want to develop

CHAPTER 10: VOCABULARY IN THE MUSIC CLASSROOM

over the entire year? You must think of each concert and piece as an educational unit, each unit building upon the skills of the previous unit while developing new skills for the future.

Play the sight-reading, and see if you are able to play through the piece after pre-teaching the skills that were lacking. I will guarantee that you and your students will feel better about their sight-reading experience. It doesn't mean that they were completely successful in playing every aspect of the piece; rather, what the students couldn't play or sing seemed feasible to be learned over time. Furthermore, it seemed possible that the students could begin working on the musical, emotional, and deeper understanding the symbols portray. Simply put, move from correcting mistakes to improving musicality.

CONCEPT OF DEFINITION MAP

A final vocabulary strategy that will help students learn musical concepts in-depth is a Concept of Definition Map. Please see Illustration 21 for an example of this map. Use this strategy when you want students to learn an important concept, one that you want them to remember ten years after they have left your classroom. For example, have students place the word "Blues" in the center circle. Now have them come up with the broader category, or what it is—a style of jazz music. Then, have students generate the properties of blues music, such as the instrumentation, the beat or key, has improvisation, etc. Then, a comparison would be another style of music, such as bee-bop, jump, etc. Finally, have students listen to and provide examples of the blues from different eras by such artists as Louis Armstrong, Muddy Waters, etc. Providing students with opportunities to explore relationships between the broader categories and the examples and properties of the concept will allow them to better understand the nuances and depth of understanding of musical concepts it takes in order to truly perform at the highest level.

ILLUSTRATION 21

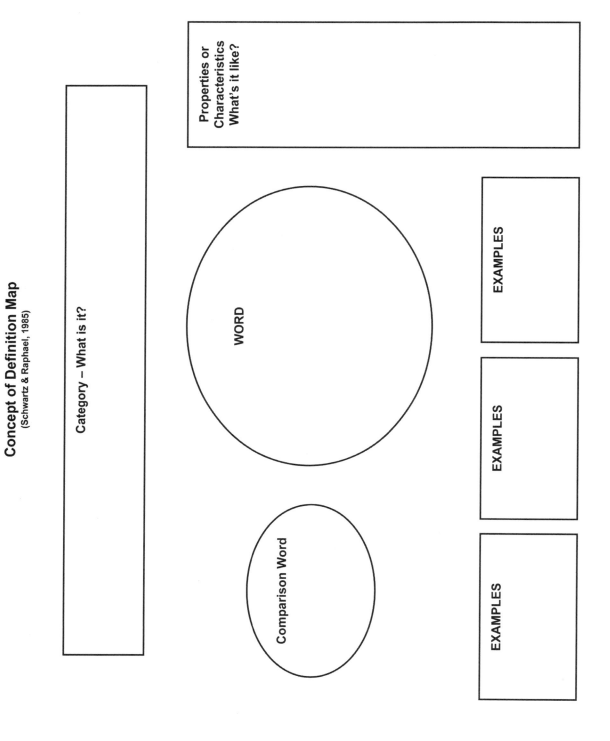

Concept of Definition Map
(Schwartz & Raphael, 1985)

Category – What is it?

Properties or
Characteristics
What's it like?

WORD

Comparison Word

EXAMPLES

EXAMPLES

EXAMPLES

CHAPTER 11
WHAT LEVEL OF MUSICAL SKILLS AND KNOWLEDGE ENHANCES A PERFORMANCE?

I hope by now that you can see that there are numerous ways to teach or reinforce a concept or skill. Let's continue by having you begin to connect musical skills and knowledge with teaching strategies. Look at the list in Illustration 22 and rank the areas from most important to least. Put a number one on the most important, followed by a two on the next, and so on until you have ranked them all. When your rankings are complete, compare your ranking with a colleague and answer the question shown in Illustration 22.

ILLUSTRATION 22

What level of musical skills or knowledge does a performer need to master in order to enhance a performance?

Ranking number	Skill	Strategy	Group Strength	Group Weakness
	Breath control			
	Vocabulary/musical terms/ symbols			
	Aural skills – interval			
	Theory, scales, intervals, keys			
	History of the pieces			
	Harmonic structure			
	Tone			
	Intonation			
	Rhythm			
	Technique			
	Interpretation/Musicianship			
	Diction, Bowing, Articulation			
	Alternate fingerings			
	Vocal – ability to read notes			
	Vocal – ability to play part on key board			
	Vocal – sing part individually using *solfége*			
	Body posture			
	Instrument position			
	Embouchure			
	Physics of sound			
	How mouthpieces work			
	How vocal chords work			

Step two in this process is to mark each area as either an ensemble strength or an ensemble weakness. Put an X in the appropriate box and, if needed, write a comment (such as flute, tenors, or violas, if this is a weakness of a particular section rather than the entire group). To support your opinion, use state contest results or festival comments from outside sources if you have them. Referring to these comments will also help you to separate what you think are strengths and weakness from what the outside world thinks.

Step three brings together the focus of the book—and that is selecting the Common Core State Standards that will enhance your teaching and reinforce the skills and content knowledge you value in order to create *Independent Musicians Creating Quality Performances*. I want you to get your copy of the Common Core State Standards and select which anchor standards you could use to enhance and reinforce the musical knowledge and skills listed in Illustration 22.

Reading

Writing

Math

In order to justify the need to use a variety of teaching strategies, next answer the following questions. These questions are designed to examine what you are doing in your classroom currently and why a different approach might help you to achieve a higher level of student understanding, accountability, and ultimately, better performances.

- What level of understanding did your students demonstrate on your last concert regarding the areas listed in Illustration 22?

- Have you ever recorded yourself in rehearsal and kept track of the comments you make and looked at the time spent on each of these areas: talking, using sarcasm, correcting, disciplining, playing, repeating comments, repeating sections, and using non-musical terms?

- How are you assessing your students' level of understanding to verify what they really learned?

- Do your students sight-read as a measure of understanding? Are they required to play a year-end jury for a panel of judges on music they had to select and prepare without any help?

Looking reflectively at one's own teaching practice is the only way to improve instruction in the classroom. And certainly, any time instruction is improved, the performance of the group will be enhanced.

CHAPTER 12
USING MATHEMATICS AND SCIENCE TO ENHANCE MUSICAL UNDERSTANDING

In the beginning of the book, I talked about my revelation about the Common Core and its foundational philosophy of in-depth learning for students. That moment also revealed music's strong connection to math and physics. Consider the ways that music educators can use math and science to help students better understand and appreciate what is expressively inherent in the music they play. Often we read an article or hear a news story about the most recent study that shows students who study music also have higher test scores in math. What would happen if we used math where appropriate to understand the connection between music and math to enhance performances while making real-world connections? The Next Generation Science Standards (http://www.nextgenscience.org) are organized by disciplinary core ideas or topics. Topics that speak closely to music are those in physical science, particularly forces and motion (PS2A), relationships between forces and motions (PS3C), and wave properties (PS4A). This Web site is very user friendly and is divided into age-appropriate standards of study.

Below are listed just a few areas related to math and physics that music educators could incorporate into their classrooms. Understanding the mathematical and physical principles at work will not only help students take responsibility for mastering musical skills, but also the scientific theories fundamental to the music. For example, intonation is one of the most pervasive problems that band, orchestra, and choir directors deal with on a daily basis. Intonation affects the balance, blend, and emotional impact of the performance and just about every aspect of a musical experience. But, have you ever thought about why groups have intonation issues? Let's look at what causes the majority of intonation problems and see if a knowledge of math, physics, writing, and research can motivate an individual to work at improving his or her intonation, and thus, impact the group's intonation. Before I give you my answers about intonation problems, generate some causes of intonation problems in a performing group. When you list them, do not rank them.

_____

_____

_____

_____

_____

_____

Now let's look at what I found were the causes for poor intonation. I will list mine in order of importance based upon which ones are easiest to fix: (1) to issues that require more student engagement in order to hear and correct intonation problems as students move from beginner to practitioner.

1. Posture
2. Horn position
3. Embouchure
4. Breath control
5. Understanding which notes on an instrument are in and out of tune and the reasons instrument designs have built-in flaws or imperfections
6. How reeds, mouthpieces, or vocal chords work
7. How to adjust slides to properly tune an instrument
8. Aural skills to hear flat and sharp notes

When asking a group of educators to rank the causes of poor intonation, each person has a different number one. For me, it is posture. Posture is directly related to horn position. A musician can't have proper instrument positioning, lung function, vocal tone production, or embouchure if posture is incorrect. If the instrument or the body is not in the proper position, then the embouchure, airflow, and overall breathing process is impaired. This issue is one that can be easily fixed, yet when it is an issue, it becomes the primary reason for intonation and other numerous problems that directors must continuously address in rehearsal. If the student is not able to produce the optimal airflow into an instrument or over the vocal chords, then the pitch or intonation will suffer. If students understood their roles in creating proper posture or horn position through looking at the physics of how sound is made in instruments and the vocal chords, then they might begin to understand that it isn't something easily fixed without them taking responsibility to demonstrate proper posture/horn position every time they play their instrument. How many comments do you make in rehearsal about proper posture? A quick and easy way to check your group's posture and horn position is to have someone take a picture of your group playing or singing. Then study the picture, looking for who is not demonstrating proper posture and horn position. Once you have the evidence, show the students the picture and then discuss what proper posture and horn position are and the reasons the students need to correct the problems. You could also have them write what happens to tone and intonation if proper posture and horn positions are not used.

Another way to address intonation problems is to look at the math and physics inherent in airflow and what happens as air flows over vocal chords, through mouthpieces, reeds, valves, and tubes. For young players, pictures and diagrams of airflow showing what happens could lead to older students doing a short research paper regarding the physics relative to their particular instrument and how posture and airflow are related. Additionally, you could work with the physics teachers in your school to make a video or to give a short presentation of the physics of sound and how it is made. The purpose of using a variety of examples from math, writing, reading, and science is so the students begin to take responsibility for playing in tune instead of the director nagging them in rehearsal. Consider the rest of the list, and think about how you could incorporate math, science, and writing to reinforce and encourage students to take a more active role in correcting intonation problems.

In Chapter 11, I asked you to list your group's musical weaknesses. I suggest you select one or two weaknesses and then explore alternative opportunities to incorporate math, writing, and physics into the music classroom. Below is a list of topics to get you started thinking about possible ways to explore math and science in the music classroom.

- Intonation
- Fractions
- Hertz
- Tuning
- Tonal system/Semi quavers
- Physics of acoustic and instruments
- Physics of acoustics and the rehearsal or performance hall
- Math and music in the Renaissance Era
- Math and Chakras
- Mouthpieces – brass
- Mouthpieces – woodwinds.
- Reeds – single and double – woodwinds
- Data on personal musical skill level
- Data on the performance group
- Statistics
- Reliability
- Validity

Answer the next few questions as you begin to apply a variety of teaching techniques, which will help you to further see the potential uses of math, science, writing, and reading.

1. How could you differentiate between the topics above for students with various levels of musical competency?
2. What are some of the areas you repeatedly have to work on in rehearsal that might benefit from a different pedagogical approach?
3. Are your students able to select areas of weaknesses they would like to improve and could you suggest new ways for them to improve?
4. What areas do you personally want to improve in your teaching? What are some ways for you to use the disciplines of math, reading, writing, and science to improve your personal goals?

By now, your mind should be full of ideas of potential areas in which you can use a variety of disciplines in the classroom. Begin this process using one selection for your next concert. Keep your efforts very specific and driven by what techniques will enhance the students' understanding of the piece and how the new approach will improve the performance of the music. Lastly, make sure you explain to the students why you are trying new approaches, how it connects music to the other disciplines in the school, and how the Common Core will help them in their future educational pursuits.

CHAPTER 13

LET'S WALK THE TALK, NOT JUST TALK THE TALK

In this chapter, we present a Unit for Musical Performance plan using music selected by directors from around the country who volunteered to provide a selection they would perform in an upcoming concert. After you have considered these examples, you will be asked in Chapter 14 to select one musical piece so that you can create your own unit plan that will incorporate the Common Core State Standards in the teaching of musical skills and content. So, begin thinking about what selection you will use. When Ann and I created these examples, we had some background knowledge about each group and the conductor. Had I created these plans for my own groups, I would have included more specific recommendations for individual students based upon past assessments of their playing ability. In the case of these examples, however, we will instead focus on the group rather than the individual level.

BAND PERFORMANCE UNIT

O Magnum Mysterium by Morten Laurisen, transcribed by H. Robert Reynolds

The previous chapters discussed the importance of selecting compositions that are focused on developing valued musical skills and improving those skills that are lacking. This piece was selected after analyzing the data from both large group and solo and ensemble contest. The comments and scores from the judges on both the individual performances and the group performances show that tone, intonation, balance, and musicality or emotion was limiting the potential of the individual and group performances. With this data in hand, *O Magnum Mysterium* was chosen to improve these skills. Primarily, the desired piece would address the skills above. The piece should also include:

- A slow tempo;
- Easier note patterns;
- Simple rhythms;
- A familiar key;
- Emotionally challenging music;
- Opportunities to develop tone, intonation, balance, blend; and
- A range that was optimal for all sections.

O Magnum Mysterium was ideal because the key is B-flat concert, the notes are almost all quarter, half, and whole notes at a slow tempo of sixty-six beats per minute. Furthermore, it was musically and emotionally challenging with a text available from the original choir setting. Both traditional teaching techniques and opportunities to embed the Common Core State Standards to correct the areas of weakness are outlined below using this piece.

1. In order to get the students to focus on the skills that were weak (tone, intonation, balance, and musicality) students were given the data and comments from their individual and group performances and were asked to write what they thought the data showed. (Common Core State Standard – Writing 1: Support a claim and use valid reasoning and relevant and sufficient evidence.) After reading their responses and tallying up the comments, the students had come to a similar conclusion about their areas of weakness. Sharing the comments with the group allowed the students to take responsibility for working both as individuals and as a group on the areas where growth was needed.

2. After discussing the student comments with the group, the ensemble goals for the next eight weeks leading up to the next concert were determined and how the director would be focusing on those skills.

3. Students then created their own goals and first weekly plan. See Illustration 6 in Chapter 5 for Planning Sheet and Illustration 7 in Chapter 5 for Weekly Reflection Sheet. Furthermore, students would write about the individual and group benefits if weaker areas were to be improved. (Common Core State Standard – Writing 1)

4. Now that the students are invested in the process of improving a performance, and they understand their role in addressing tone, intonation, balance, and musicality, the director can began the pre-teaching of the selection by having students complete a Music Vocabulary Knowledge Rating sheet. See Illustration 23. (Common Core State Standard – Language 4, 5, and 6)

ILLUSTRATION 23

Music Vocabulary Knowledge Rating Sheet

Word/Rhythm	Page/Measure #	No Clue	Seen or Heard	Can Define and Demonstrate Symbol
O Magnum Mysterium				
Adagio, molto legato e espressivo				
Quarter = 66-72				
4/4				
3/2				
Rit,				
P				
A Tempo				
Concert Eb				
Concert D				
mp				
Crescendo				
mf				
mp				
Diminuendo				
Fermata				
pp				
Poco rit.				
tutti				
A tempo, deliberamente				
Molto rit.				
ff				
lunga				
Latin language				

5. After reviewing the answers from the initial Music Vocabulary Knowledge Rating Scale, the words *deliberamente, lunga, expressive,* and the *a tempo* marking of 66 beats per minute were words that spoke directly to the musicality or emotion of the composition. Thus, it was determined to have students play the scale with the metronome, holding each note out for eight beats and having them focus on

intonation and tone quality. Because the piece requires the musicians to play long, tied whole notes that *crescendo* and *diminuendo,* the students should focus on that skill before playing the piece. In addition, the three words, *deliberamente, lunga, and expressive* were written on the board and students were asked to demonstrate those words by playing a scale. (Common Core State Standard–Reading in Science and Technical Subjects – 4: Determine the meaning of symbols, key terms, and other domain-specific words and phrases as they are used in a specific context.)

6. Finally, students would write what they would have to perform physically on their instrument in order to produce the notes as demanded by the musical terms. (Common Core State Standard – Writing 1) Student responses included breath support, airflow, listening, center tone, posture, horn position, and mental concentration. They had begun to grasp the concept that in order to play emotionally, musicians need to think emotionally and understand what an emotion would sound like when played by an instrument.

7. Students then were assigned to find recordings of either popular or Classical music that elicited emotional feelings. Students could use a three-column note format (See Illustration 24) to record the sections and the emotion they believe as they listened to the piece. (Common Core State Standard – Writing 1) Students could volunteer to bring in the examples they found, thus providing the beginning of each rehearsal for the next week with one short example they had found. The opportunity for hearing a variety of music and rich discussion was a key toward having students gain an in-depth understanding of musicality. After discussing the emotion, the students could then duplicate that emotion, if possible, on a chorale or on a scale in the key of *O Magnum Mysterium.*

8. Text from the original choir arrangement was handed out, with the Latin on one side and the English translation on the other. Students were asked to write what they thought the text was about and where would a text like this be used. (Common Core State Standard, Reading1)

O magnum mysterium,	O great mystery
Et admirable sacramentum	And wondrous sacrament
Ut animalia viderent Dominum Natum,	That animals should see the new-born Lord,
jacentum in praespeio	lying in their manger
Beata Virgo, cujus viscera	Blessed is the virgin whose womb
Meruerunt portare	Was worthy to bear the
Dominum christum. Alleluia!	Lord Jesus Christ. Alleluia!

9. To connect the text and the need for the group to mimic a choir, the original choir music was projected on a screen in the band room and a recording of a choir was played as the students followed the choral arrangement. Again, students were asked to write a short response about how the musical interpretation supported the meaning of the text. (Common Core State Standard – Writing 1)

10. The above steps took one week and only about five to ten minutes a day. Now it was time to hand out the band arrangement and play through the selection. Having listened to emotional intensity in pieces and demonstrating that type of playing in numerous settings from chorales to scales, the students were able to play the dynamics of the piece on the first reading with emotion, focused tone, and correct intonation.

11. Because this selection is very chordal, the music theory explaining the triads, inversions, intervals, and suspensions, and the use of dissonance were investigated during rehearsals. This type of learning allowed students to gain a more in-depth understanding of the music and how composers use musical techniques for greater musical impact.

12. The student Planning Sheet and Weekly Reflection (See Illustration 6 and 7 in Chapter 5) were completed weekly and the Rehearsal Plan and Review Sheet (See Illustration 8 and 9 in Chapter 5) was used every other week as a check as a further check for understanding. (Common Core State Standard – Writing 1)

13. After the concert, the ensemble reflected on the process and what they thought had been accomplished before beginning selection of skill targets and music for the next concert. (Common Core State Standard – Writing 1)

The above example is only a snapshot of how embedding Common Core State Standards can assist a group in setting and meeting musical content and skill goals. Now, it is your turn to find one selection for your next concert that will improve your ensemble and focus you and your students on improving a skill that will get you off the performance treadmill and on the road to a higher level of musical performance for your group.

ILLUSTRATION 24

Title & Section	Emotion	Explanation

CHOIR PERFORMANCE UNIT

The Stars Stand Up In the Air by Eric William Barnum

When a local high school choir director gave me this piece, I could immediately see the possibilities of combining traditional teaching strategies with opportunities to embed Common Core State Standards to enhance student musical understanding. Based upon a previous assessment of student strengths and weaknesses, the primary goal for the unit was to have students understand the relationship of text to musicality in a choral piece. Students also needed to focus on their understanding of rhythm, scales, and *solfége*.

1. Before distributing the piece, and to get a more specific grasp of the students' understanding of the musical terms and concepts within this piece, students were given a Music Vocabulary Knowledge Rating Sheet. See Illustration 25.

ILLUSTRATION 25

Word/Rhythm	Page/Measure #	No Clue	Seen or Heard	Can Define and Demonstrate Symbol
Quarter note = 66	m-1			
Quarter note = 96	m-6			
Quarter note = 88	m-38			
Quarter note = 64	m-64			
Quarter note = 76	m-67			
3/4	m-1			
2/4	m-63			
4/4	m-64			
With great Longing	m-1			
rallentando				
Key with 2 # #				
A tempo				
Poco rall.				
Tenuto.				
Poco accel.				
Piu mosso				
Subito f				
Tempo 1				
4/4				
Pp cresc, poco a poco al f				
Molto rallentando				

2. Based upon results from this Rating Scale, instruction needed to be focused on the following:

   a. Metronome markings and how they relate to mathematics (Common Core Mathematics Standards – Number Systems) and time.

   b. The key of D and its minor B and how solfége could be used to learn this concept. Teaching students to play this scale on a piano would also provide students with another opportunity for developing skills for reading musical notation. Free keyboard apps would help students understand the relationship between notes on a keyboard and on the written page. The ability to find beginning pitches on a keyboard, to use *solfége*, and for the more advanced students, to be able to play parts during practice sessions will allow students to become independent musicians. Additionally, students could respond to the prompt, "How can learning to read notes and play the key board benefit choral musicians?" (Common Core State Standards – Writing 1)

   c. The musical terms used in the piece. These terms should be listed on the board and reinforced when singing warm-ups and scales. Students should be asked, both individually and as a group, to *crescendo, decresendo, rallentando,* and *accelerando* while singing these exercises. For example, have the following instructions on the board: Sing the scale D up and down, repeating the top note and using solfége. *Crescendo* going up and *diminuendo* coming down while performing a *rallentando* to the last note. The group could sing it first, followed by individuals.

3. *The Stars Stand Up In the Air* is based upon a poem by the Irish poet Thomas MacDonaugh. Understanding the intent of the poet is crucial to being able to sing this piece with musical intensity; it also requires a few activities prior to rehearsal in order for students to understand the words to the music. Therefore, before distributing the piece, write the statement on the board, "Is it better to have loved and lost, or never loved at all?" Students can do a Think, Pair, Share where they write their individual reactions to the statement, then share with a partner before discussing with the group. (Common Core State Standard – Writing 1) This activity will activate student background knowledge as to the grief of losing a loved one and thus, they will be better able to understand the perspective of the poet, allowing them to sing with greater emotional capacity. After discussing of the students' opinions on the topic of love and loss, provide them with the actual poem:

The stars stand up in the air,
The sun and the moon are gone,
The strand of its waters is bare,
And her sway is swept from the swan.

The cuckoo was calling all day,
Hid in the branches above,
How my stoirin is fled away,
'Tis my grief that I gave her my love.

Three things through love I see –
Sorrow and sin and death –
And my mind reminding me
That this doom I breathe with my breath.

But sweeter than violin or lute
Is my love – and she left me behind.
I wish that all music were mute,
And I to all beauty were blind

She's more shapely than swan by the strand,
She's more radiant than grass after dew,
She's more fair than the stars where they stand –
'tis my grief that her ever I knew!

After students have read the poem, have them find evidence in the text to support the theme of *Is it better to have loved and lost, than never to have loved at all?* (Common Core State Standard – Reading 1) Taking the time to have students better understand the text will result in greater musical understanding and an enhanced musical performance.

4. Now distribute the piece and read the text in rhythm without playing the pitches, saying the words. I call this intoning or speak/singing.

5. Count the song the same way. Using a consistent counting method, ensure by pre-teaching, that students understand all the rhythms. Reinforce the power of being able to accurately read the music rhythmically as a group and individually. Again, the ability to read music will give students the tools to be independent and be able to practice not only at school, but also at home.

6. Play the accompaniment while students hum and read their parts. In this piece, the piano has running eighth notes and numerous chords under the vocalists' moving parts.

7. Students are now ready to sing the selection in sections with the accompaniment. The goal is to sing through sections without major stopping. Remember the saying, "If they can't sing straight through the piece, then it is too hard."

8. Lastly, the director should hand out the Planning and Reflection Sheets so that students can articulate their plans to practice individually at home. (See Illustrations 6 and 7 in Chapter 5.) These sheets are a must for choirs so that the time in rehearsal is spent on getting to the music and not teaching by rote. Rote teaching has no long-term benefit for students, because they never are able to read music on their own. It is time to create musicians who are able to read and sing music independently.

Overall, the potential for teaching chords, triads, inversions, and intervals, in addition to music history, is infinite. Regardless of what compositions you choose, greater musical understanding and higher-level performance skills will be the result of your efforts.

ORCHESTRA PERFORMANCE UNIT

Bavarian Rhapsody by David Shaffer

As with the band and choral ensembles, *Bavarian Rhapsody* was selected with the intention of developing the musical skills that were valued at this particular school and needed strengthening: intonation, balance, and blend. The director also wanted the students to understand how triads and inversions are used within a composition to create emotional intensity. If the students had a better understanding of triads, then working on balance and blend would increase their understanding of the role they played in creating a chord. Knowledge of triads would also allow the musicians to concentrate on intonation and finger and hand position. This orchestra is composed mainly of freshmen of varying skill abilities that come from three middle schools. Therefore, the selection would take into consideration:

- Simple rhythms with no sixteenth notes;
- Familiar key, either major or minor;
- Four clearly defined parts;
- Score that includes a piano part that could be used in a discussions of chords;
- Tempo less than 120 beats per minute; and
- Instrument range limited to students' current ability.

Bavarian Rhapsody, which is in the key of e minor and has a tempo of 120 or less, met the above criteria that would allow students to work on intonation, balance, and blend.

To introduce the skill focus, the ensemble listened to a previous concert. Students identified the strengths and the weaknesses they heard in their group and created a list. Then they listened to a recording of the same piece played by a more mature group. Again, they reflected on the performance and wrote down the strengths and weaknesses. Finally, students were asked to compare the performances of the two groups on a Venn Diagram. (Common Core State Standard – Reading 7: Integrate and evaluate content presented in diverse media and formats.) The students shared their opinions, and overwhelmingly, they listed balance, blend and intonation as skills that needed to be strengthened. Following that discussion, the group brainstormed causes for those problems, citing finger position, hand position, bow position, body posture, and instrument position as possible causes of poor intonation. From this discussion, the group began to see their role in correcting poor positions and posture. Now that the students were invested, the director began the pre-teaching of the selection by handing out the Music Vocabulary Knowledge Rating Sheet. (See Illustration 26 in Chapter 10)

ILLUSTRATION 26

Music Vocabulary Knowledge Rating Sheet

Word/Rhythm	Page/Measure #	No Clue	Seen or Heard	Can Define and Demonstrate Symbol
Bavarian				
Rhapsody				
Quarter note = 120				
Quarter note = 60				
Quarter note = 78				
Quarter note = 56				
4/4				
A Tempo				
Concert G				
e- harmonic minor				
Brisk				
Pizz				
Arco				
Marcato				
Molto accel.				
Expressive				
F				
Ff				
Mf				
Pp				
Triad				
Inversion				
Balance				
Interval				

1. To begin teaching how triads function, the group played the major scale of G upon which *Bavarian Rhapsody* is based. Students counted off by ones, threes, and fives. A common warm-up for some groups is to have the ones begin the scale, holding out each note until signaled by the director to move up the scale to the next note. The ones would play the first two notes and then on the third note,

group three would start on the first note of the scale. Both the ones and threes would move up together on different notes for two more notes. When the ones got to the fifth note, and the threes were on the third note, the fives would play the first note of the scale, forming a triad. Because the students were numbered one, three or five, regardless of section, every group of three students formed their own triad. This partnership compelled them to listen to how each individual note blended as part of the triad. Thus, students could hear the triads up and down the scale, forming major, minor and diminished chords as they continued to move up and down the scale before all returned to the starting note of G. It was important for the students not to read the triads; instead, they had to play and listen. The reading and writing of triads would come later in the year and was not the focus of this unit

2. The group played the triad scale for several rehearsals before playing the e-minor harmonic scale in the same fashion. Since the scale was in a minor key, students were able to hear the difference between major and minor. At the end of the minor scale warm-up, two chorales were played, one major and the other minor. Students were asked to write the differences that they heard using musical terms that were posted on the board. Additionally, the students were given an outside assignment to find an example of a song written in major and another song written in minor. The style or genre of the piece they found did not matter. Once they chose a selection, they wrote a short paragraph about why they thought the pieces were major and minor and what the differences were. This writing was based solely upon their listening experience. (Common Core State Standard – Writing 1)

3. The next step was to discuss why composers use triads. A simple chorale was projected on the board with chord numbers written beneath. The students then played the chorale and the notes were discussed regarding which chords were in a root position and which were inversions. A discussion ensued about what happens when the third of a triad moves above the fifth. Once the students understood that the third of a triad is difficult to hear in a root position, and that they must play that note a bit stronger to balance the triad, they began to realize what they had to do to improve the balance and blend of the ensemble.

4. *Bavarian Rhapsody* was handed out and sight-read. The first reading was successful because the group had spent time working on balance and blend in the same key as the piece, and they had learned to adjust their playing depending upon what part of a chord they played.

5. In order to further understand this selection, a discussion about Bavarian music followed and what constituted a rhapsody. Students were asked to find one other song with the word rhapsody in it and compare it to the one they were playing,

thus enhancing their overall knowledge of the genre. They were given a word bank, or a list of musical terms, they could incorporate into their short compare and contrast assignment. (Common Core State Standards – Writing 2: Write informative or explanatory texts.)

6. Throughout the eight weeks, the Planning Sheet and the Weekly Reflection Sheet (See Illustrations 6 and 7 in Chapter 5, respectively) were used to help the students meet their goal of improving intonation, balance and blend. The Rehearsal Review and Plan Sheet (See Illustration 8 and 9 in Chapter 5) were used every other week to further ensure that they were accomplishing their goal as a group.

7. After the performance, students listened to a piece of music from the concert from the previous year that showed weak intonation, balance, and blend. Then they listened to the performance of *Bavarian Rhapsody*. Students were asked to compare the two performances and note areas of improvement. (Common Core State Standard – Writing 2). With a focused effort to strengthen skills, improvement was robust, providing both students and their director with tangible evidence of progress toward goals.

Targeting weak areas in rehearsals and adjusting instruction to address those skills is very powerful. Allowing students to witness their growth in musical skills and knowledge is a great motivator. I hope you will select just one piece for your next concert and develop your own focused rehearsals that incorporate Common Core State Standards to enhance your students' performance skills.

GENERAL MUSIC UNIT

General music teachers can certainly encourage student appreciation of music by including the Common Core State Standards in their music lessons and by encouraging students to read outside of class. One of the ways to do this is to include books that have a musical theme into the classroom. For example, a book in the *Adventures with Music* series published by GIA Publications, Inc., features students learning to play the blues. One activity that develops an understanding of that musical genre is a Concept of Definition map. (Common Core State Standard – Language 5) See Illustration 21 for an example of a Concept of Definition Map. Students would then place the word "Blues" in the center circle. The teacher would then have students figure out the broader category, or what it is—a style of jazz music. Next the students would generate the properties of blues music, such as the instrumentation, the beat or key, has improvisation, etc. A comparison word would be another style of music, such as hip hop, rap, etc. Finally, students could listen to and provide examples of the Blues from different eras by such artists as Louis Armstrong, Muddy Waters, etc.

Additionally, general music teachers can guide students toward themes that support the value of music in a person's life. An example of a theme for *Dog Tags* from the *Adventures with Music* series is that hard work and practice pays off. Students would then find four examples in the text that support this theme. (Common Core State Standard – Reading 2) In reflection, the more connections music teachers can make between the music classroom and the students' outside world, the greater the chance that students will become lifelong, knowledgeable supporters of the arts.

CHAPTER 14
YOUR TURN

When Ann and I discussed how to make this book more relevant and usable, the chapter called YOUR TURN was born. We wanted more than just concepts and ideas; we both wanted Chapter 13 to include examples of how to implement a Unit for Musical Performance and Chapter 14 to walk the reader through the process of creating a unit plan, using one of their own selections. Yes, just one. No matter what time of year you are reading this chapter, begin to think about your next concert or unit. Go through the process discussed in this book and incorporate the Common Core State Standards into a unit design for a piece of music you are planning to play. The steps below and the accompanying blackline masters in the appendix have been discussed throughout the previous chapters. Refer back to the chapters when needed and try creating your own unit plan. Start on a selection that you feel will develop the musical skills that are valued in your program that will motivate you to try something new. Talk to your administration about your plan to incorporate the Common Core State Standards into your classroom, and ask them what kind of supports there are to help you.

One of my favorite quotes that I used in a previous book will guide your journey.

Yesterday is gone. Tomorrow has not yet come. We have only today. Let us begin.

Mother Teresa (1910–1997)
Missionary and winner of the Nobel Peace Prize

Let's begin.

SIX STEPS IN HOW TO DESIGN A UNIT FOR A MUSICAL PERFORMANCE

Once the knowledge and skills have been determined, the levels of mastery set, and the assessments created, the teacher can begin to design a unit for a musical performance class. The following six steps are key to the process of an effectively designed unit.

ILLUSTRATION 27

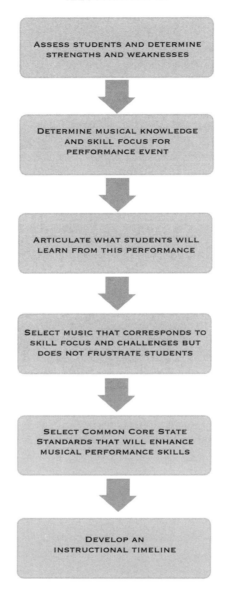

CHAPTER 15

FREQUENTLY ASKED QUESTIONS

1. **How do I get started? This task seems overwhelming.**

    You start with baby steps. It has been a common thread throughout this book that you start with one composition. No matter the time of year, select a piece and use the process outlined in Chapters 5, 6, and 7. And then you begin. Once you have selected your piece, be sure to explain to your students, parents and administration what you are implementing and why. Your administration will applaud your efforts. You and your students will begin to see the power in the time spent on Common Core State Standards that are used to enhance musical performance while supporting and developing the whole student.

2. **Won't a focus on reading and writing take away from my rehearsal time?**

    Any time you begin something for the first time, you may lose some rehearsal time. But, in the long run, time spent on the writing and reading Common Core State Standards will pay dividends in the future. You will have more focused student independent practice sessions, and rehearsals that are more efficient and allow students to learn the music in depth. Finally, you will have more time to spend with family and other activities because you are not seen as the sole driving force behind the group. You have created an army of musicians who independently prepare music outside of rehearsal. Oh, what a feeling!

3. **How do I get my department to do this together?**

    Collaboration comes from sitting together with your colleagues and administration and discussing what the group values, not what the individual values. This may seem blunt, but each member of your faculty will eventually retire or die. The school and the programs, however, will continue, and that should be the focus. What musical skills and concepts should the students learn regardless of who is the teacher? This is a question that a department needs to discuss. Music programs should avoid being driven by a single teacher's opinion, especially if it is at the expense of the students.

4. **My students want to play not write; won't they rebel?**

    Don't short change or underestimate your students. If students can see through your example the power of inherent writing, and learning musical skills in depth, they will not complain. The complaining usually comes from unfocused and unconnected musical experiences. Making real-world connections to what is going on in the world allows students to further understand how music fits into the bigger picture.

5. **How do I blend reading, writing, listening theory, written theory, and performance skills all into one grade?**

   The easiest answer is read the book *Grading for Musical Excellence*, which is completely devoted to answering this question. The other answer is that your grades should reflect students' musical growth. Using writing or other methods to reinforce that goal is not the focus of your grades, but it is a way to have your students articulate their understanding of musical concepts and their perception of their skills. Find a balance so your students see the importance of writing in the music classroom while keeping the grade based upon music understanding and demonstration of skills. Additionally, non-musical activities should not be included in the grade such as attendance, attitude, participation, and effort.

6. **I am not an English teacher, so how will I grade the students' writing?**

   Chapter 8 contains a discussion about ways to provide feedback to students concerning their writing. We don't expect you to be an English teacher or grade according to their grading criteria. If the students are able to clearly communicate, then keep your comments focused on the musical content and not necessarily the mechanics. As the year progresses, you may want to discuss the importance of spelling or grammar as a way of enhancing communication, but the initial focus should be on the musical content of the writing. You are the expert in this area, and an English teacher would feel just as leery about commenting on musical content in their classes. Furthermore, don't forget your school's English or language arts teachers may have rubrics that are familiar to students that could be helpful in providing feedback to students.

7. **I don't have time to grade papers.**

   Each day has twenty-four hours. I do think you will have to find some time to read student reflections, reviews, or other writings, but I also think you should have peers reading one another's writing. Make sure your student writing assignments are meaningful, short, and on topics that improve performance. Determine a way to make the process of writing and reading manageable. I think time is everywhere around us, we just have to decide how to use it to our advantage and not make it an excuse for not improving our students' performances in different and meaningful ways.

8. **How often should students write?**

    A weekly plan and review are a must and should be done outside of class. The rehearsal review sheet should be spaced out to help you and your students reflect on rehearsals and refocus effort. Other writing prompts should be used when appropriate and balanced between in-class (short) and out-of-class assignments that require more thought and effort. I cannot recommend a set number because it depends on how you want to improve an area of weakness or enhance strengths. The time spent on writing will also depend upon the class.

9. **Will I be held accountable for students who demonstrate poor writing skills?**

    Each school is different, but the majority of schools are not holding music teachers accountable for improving writing skills. You may be held accountable for having students write, but the main responsibility for a music educator is to measure individual and group musical growth by providing multiple methods of assessment.

10. **How will I use the Common Core to show growth on musical skills?**

    First, you should have a baseline for each student regarding their level of mastery on musical skills and knowledge that you value. How you move the students from one level to another would show that you use a variety of teaching techniques, including performance and writing. Everyone learns in a variety of ways. Incorporating the Common Core State Standards into the music classroom will provide you with an additional opportunity for students to showcase musical skills. Showing your students, parents, and administration that you are using a variety of methods to help students learn will reinforce a philosophy that music should be a part of every student's education.

CHAPTER 16

RECAPITULATION: CONNECTING MUSICAL UNDERSTANDING AND SKILLS TO THE BIGGER PICTURE

The only way to make sense out of change is to plunge into it, move with it, and join the dance.
—Alan Watts

The above quote by Alan Watts sums up the essence of what this book is about and what music education needs to do to survive in a fast-changing educational environment. Change is at first uncomfortable, but as you witness the growth and the improved performance abilities of your students by implementing the Common Core State Standards, you will feel a renewed sense of excitement each day you teach. Being seen by parents, teachers, colleagues, administrators, and finally your students as a teacher who values developing the whole child will be life changing. We have the chance to be the agents of change in justifying why music education should be a vital part of a child's education. Connecting our discipline by focusing our teaching on in-depth understanding using the Common Core will further justify music to your school and community. We hope this book has opened your mind to a new way of thinking about how to develop *Independent Musicians Creating Quality Performances*. Having students taking more responsibility for learning and demonstrating the musical skills you value will be the first step in creating the next generation of adults who will mandate that music be an integral part of our schools, having seen the connection between music and twenty-first-century skills.

We congratulate you for reading and implementing the ideas in this book. This step is only the beginning of the evolution of your teaching practice, but all journeys must begin somewhere and that somewhere is now. We hope that you will share your successes with us by sending us e-mails and posting your questions on our Web site: www.mpae.net. Be sure to contact us if you would like the files for the blackline masters that you can edit and adjust to your school's particular needs. Your journey is our journey, and we want to support you in any way we can. Share your work with your administration, parents, and especially your colleagues so that we can begin to show the world that music educators are leaders and that music is a subject that develops the total person. Enjoy!

"A Richer, Fuller Life Through Music!"

Appendices

A

P21 Framework for 21st Century Learning (Skills, 2009)
The Partnership for 21st Century Skills has developed a vision for student success in the new global economy.

21ST CENTURY STUDENT OUTCOMES

To help practitioners integrate skills into the teaching of core academic subjects, the Partnership has developed a unified, collective vision for learning known as the Framework for 21st Century Learning. This Framework describes the skills, knowledge and expertise students must master to succeed in work and life; it is a blend of content knowledge, specific skills, expertise, and literacies.

Every 21st century skills implementation requires the development of core academic subject knowledge and understanding among all students. Those who can think critically and communicate effectively must build on a base of core academic subject knowledge. Within the context of core knowledge instruction, **students must also learn the essential skills for success in today's world, such as critical thinking, problem solving, communication, and collaboration.**

When a school or district builds on this foundation, combining the entire Framework with the necessary support systems—standards, assessments, curriculum and instruction, professional development and learning environments—students are more engaged in the learning process and graduate better prepared to thrive in today's global economy.

Core Subjects and 21st Century Themes

Mastery of **core subjects and 21st century themes** is essential to student success. Core subjects include English, reading or language arts, world languages, arts, mathematics, economics, science, geography, history, government, and civics.

In addition, schools must promote an understanding of academic content at much higher levels by weaving **21st century interdisciplinary themes** into core subjects:

- Global Awareness
- Financial, Economic, Business, and Entrepreneurial Literacy
- Civic Literacy
- Health Literacy
- Environmental Literacy

Learning and Innovation Skills

Learning and innovation skills are what separate students who are prepared for increasingly complex life and work environments in today's world and those who are not. They include:

- Creativity and Innovation
- Critical Thinking and Problem Solving
- Communication and Collaboration

Information, Media and Technology Skills

Today, we live in a technology and media-driven environment, marked by access to an abundance of information, rapid changes in technology tools and the ability to collaborate and make individual contributions on an unprecedented scale. Effective citizens and workers must be able to exhibit a range of functional and critical thinking skills, such as:

- Information Literacy
- Media Literacy
- ICT (Information, Communications and Technology) Literacy

Life and Career Skills

Today's life and work environments require far more than thinking skills and content knowledge. The ability to navigate the complex life and work environments in the globally competitive information age requires students to pay rigorous attention to developing adequate life and career skills, such as:

- Flexibility and Adaptability
- Initiative and Self-Direction
- Social and Cross-Cultural Skills
- Productivity and Accountability
- Leadership and Responsibility

B

ENGLISH LANGUAGE ARTS COMMON CORE ANCHOR STANDARDS IN READING

KEY IDEAS AND DETAILS

1. Read closely to determine what the text says explicitly and to make logical inferences from it; cite specific textual evidence when writing or speaking to support conclusions drawn from the text.
2. Determine central ideas or themes of a text and analyze their development; summarize the key supporting details and ideas.
3. Analyze how and why individuals, events, and ideas develop and interact over the course of a text.

CRAFT AND STRUCTURE

1. Interpret words and phrases as they are used in a text, including determining technical, connotative, and figurative meanings, and analyze how specific word choices shape meaning or tone.
2. Analyze the structure of texts, including how specific sentences, paragraphs, and larger portions of the text e.g., a section, chapter, scene, or stanza relate to each other and the whole.
3. Assess how point of view or purpose shapes the content and style of a text.

INTEGRATION OF KNOWLEDGE AND IDEAS

1. Integrate and evaluate content presented in diverse formats and media, including visually and quantitatively, and in words.
2. Delineate and evaluate the argument and specific claims in a text, including the validity of the reasoning as well as the relevance and sufficiency of the evidence.
3. Analyze how two or more texts address similar themes or topics in order to build knowledge or to compare the approaches the authors take.

RANGE OF READING AND LEVEL OF TEXT COMPLEXITY

1. Read and comprehend complex literary and informational texts independently and proficiently.

C

ENGLISH LANGUAGE ARTS COMMON CORE ANCHOR STANDARDS IN WRITING

TEXT TYPES AND PURPOSES

1. Write arguments to support claims in an analysis of substantive topics or texts using valid reasoning and relevant and sufficient evidence.
2. Write informative/explanatory texts to examine and convey complex ideas and information clearly and accurately through the effective selection, organization, and analysis of content.
3. Write narratives to develop real or imagined experiences or events using effective technique, well-chosen details and well-structured event sequences.

PRODUCTION AND DISTRIBUTION OF WRITING

1. Produce clear and coherent writing in which the development, organization, and style are appropriate to task, purpose, and audience.
2. Develop and strengthen writing as needed by planning, revising, editing, rewriting, or trying a new approach.
3. Use technology, including the Internet, to produce and publish writing and to interact and collaborate with others.

RESEARCH TO BUILD AND PRESENT KNOWLEDGE

1. Conduct short as well as more sustained research projects based on focused questions, demonstrating understanding of the subject under investigation.
2. Gather relevant information from multiple print and digital sources, assess the credibility and accuracy of each source, and integrate the information while avoiding plagiarism.
3. Draw evidence from literary or informational texts to support analysis, reflection, and research.

RANGE OF WRITING

1. Write routinely over extended time frames (time for research, reflection, and revision) and shorter time frames (a single sitting or a day or two) for a range of tasks, purposes, and audiences.

BLACKLINE MASTERS

Description

Name:_____   Date:_____

| Example | Example |

| Example | Example |

Topic

Sequence

Name:_____   Date:_____

Step 1

⇩

Step 2

⇩

Step 3

⇩

Step 4

⇩

Step 5

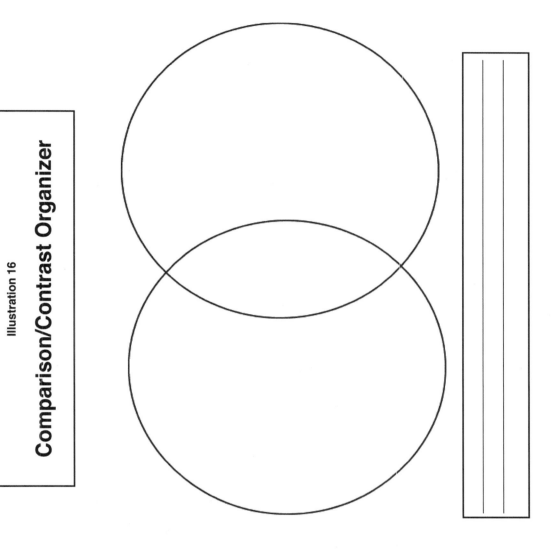

Illustration 16

Comparison/Contrast Organizer

Problem – Solution

Name:_____   Date:_____

Problem or Conflict

Possible Solution	Possible Solution	Possible Solution
Pros	Pros	Pros
Cons	Cons	Cons

Final Solution

Cause - Effect

Name:_____   Date:_____

Opinion – Proof/Argumentative Writing

Name:_____   Date:_____

Topic: What issue do you want to address?

What is your opinion about the issue?

What is your evidence?

List two supporting facts

1.

2.

What is your evidence?

List two supporting facts

1.

2.

Conclusion: What would you like the person to do?

Music Vocabulary Knowledge Rating Sheet

Name_____

Word/Rhythm	Page/ Mea- sure #	No Clue	Seen or Heard	Can Define and Demonstrate Symbol

PLANNING SHEET

This plan sheet should focus on what areas in the music you need to work on. Times and dates should be accurate. Please use music-specific language.

Name_____Due Date_____ Student ID_____

LUCK – There is no such thing as luck; only the ability to
LABOR – UNDER – CORRECT – KNOWLEDGE

Friday – Date____Start Time_____End Time_____

Band/Perc./Ensemble/Solo/Lesson/Scale   Section/Measures What is the focus?

Saturday – Date____ Start Time_____End Time_____

Band/Perc./Ensemble/Solo/Lesson/Scale   Section/Measures What is the focus?

Sunday – Date____ Start Time_____End Time_____

Band/Perc./Ensemble/Solo/Lesson/Scale   Section/Measures What is the focus?

Monday – Date____ Start Time_____End Time_____

Band/Perc./Ensemble/Solo/Lesson/Scale   Section/Measures What is the focus?

Tuesday – Date____ Start Time_____End Time_____

Band/Perc./Ensemble/Solo/Lesson/Scale   Section/Measures What is the focus?

Wednesday – Date____ Start Time_____End Time_____

Band/Perc./Ensemble/Solo/Lesson/Scale   Section/Measures What is the focus?

Thursday – Date____ Start Time_____End Time_____

Band/Percussion./Ensemble/Solo/Lesson/Scale Section/Measures What is the focus?

Rehearsal Review and Plan Sheet

Name_____Date_____Week #_____

Title of Piece_____

The instructions are on the reverse side of this form.

Comments about correctives or basic musical skills

1.

2.

3.

Comments about higher-level musical understanding
1.

2.

3.

Based upon the comments above, are there areas that you should strengthen in your playing? If you need to take responsibility for moving the group from basic corrections to a higher level, musically oriented rehearsal, what will you do this next week in your practice? Be specific in what measure or skill needs to be worked on.

1.

2.

3.

WEEKLY REFLECTION SHEET

Name_____ Date_____

Review sheets are designed for you to reflect back on your planning sheet to see if you have accomplished what you had written previously. Use this reflective time to review goals and gain insight into your weekly accomplishments.

You must have correct dates of missed goals, specific bars not worked on, and make-up work. Answers must be in depth and not one-word answers.

The purpose of this assignment is for you to be honest with yourself and understand why you are or are not reaching your written goals. If you learn how to turn negative behavior into positive behavior, you will have a have a greater chance to reach your goals.

How many practice times did you schedule?_____

How many times did you actually practice?_____

If you missed some planned practice times – Explain Be specific.

List the sections in your music you need to work on for the next performance:

Title   **Section/Measure**   **What is the focus?**

Could you have planned better to reach this week's goals? Yes – No: Explain

What will you do differently next week? You must be specific.

RESOURCES AND REFERENCES

Berger, John. (2013) *Contagious, Why Things Catch On*, Simon & Schuster, New York.

Dean, Ceri B., Elizabeth Ross Hubbell, Howard Pitler, B.J. Stone. (2012) *Classroom Instruction that Works*, 2nd Edition. ASCD, Alexandria, Virginia.

Deci, Edward L. and Richard Flast. (1996) *Why We Do What We Do: Understanding Self-Motivation*. Penguin Books, New York.

Delong, Thomas J. (2011) *Flying Without a Net, Turn Fear of Change into Fuel for Success*. Harvard Business Review Press, Boston, Massachusetts.

Dweck, Carol S. (2008) *Mindset: The New Psychology of Success*. Ballantine Books, New York.

Solis, Brian. (2013) *What's The Future of Business, Changing the Way Businesses Create Experiences*. John Wiley & Sons Inc., Hoboken, New Jersey.

About the Authors

A music educator for thirty-three years, **Paul Kimpton** recently retired from his position as director of bands and department chairman at a suburban Chicago high school, where the music program was known for its innovation and high performance standards. Mr. Kimpton received his bachelor's and master's in music education from the University of Illinois, an Administrator's Certificate from Western Illinois University and a Guidance/Counseling Certificate from Northern Illinois University.

Kimpton is the co-author of the best-selling music books, *Scale Your Way to Music Assessment* and *Grading For Musical Excellence*. Along with his wife, Ann, he is the author of the *Adventures with Music Series* books, *Starting Early, Dog Tags, Summer of Firsts,* and *Stepping Up* published by GIA Publications, Inc.. Additionally, Paul Kimpton has written articles for *The Instrumentalist*, the *Illinois Music Educator* magazine and is on the advisory board for the Illinois High School Association. He is a valued clinician on music assessment and grading throughout the United States and Canada in addition to traveling North America giving author talks to schools. He was honored with the Outstanding Music Educator Award from the National Federation of High Schools.

Ann Kaczkowski Kimpton is an assistant principal for curriculum and instruction and former literacy department chair and teacher at a suburban Chicago high school. Mrs. Kimpton received her bachelor's in English and journalism from the University of Illinois, a master's degree in reading and an Administrator's Certificate from Northern Illinois University, and has completed the coursework in curriculum and instruction for a doctoral degree. She has given numerous presentations and workshops at the local, state, and national level, and is in constant demand as an expert in literacy.

An accomplished musician, Mrs. Kimpton played French horn in the University of Illinois Symphonic Bands under the direction of Dr. Harry Begian, and she is a color guard specialist for marching bands. You might also recognize her as the mother in the Yamaha Music band recruitment video, *The Great Beginning*.

Other Published Works

The Podium Series
Changing Music Education One Book at a Time

Scale Your Way to Music Assessment
Grading for Musical Excellence:
Putting Music Back Into Your Grades

Coming Soon

Stepping Off the Podium

Additional Books by the Authors Available through giamusic.com

Also available in the *Adventures with Music* series

#1 – *Starting Early:*
A Boy and His Bugle in America During WWII

Curriculum Guide to *Starting Early*

#2 – *Dog Tags:*
A Young Musician's Sacrifice During WWII

Curriculum Guide to *Dog Tags*

#3 – *A Summer of Firsts:*
WW II Is Ending, But the Music Adventures are Just Beginning

Curriculum Guide to *A Summer of Firsts*

#4 – *Stepping Up:*
WW II Is Over, But a Young Musician Must Learn to Fight His Own Battles

For more information or to contact the authors, visit www.adventureswithmusic.net